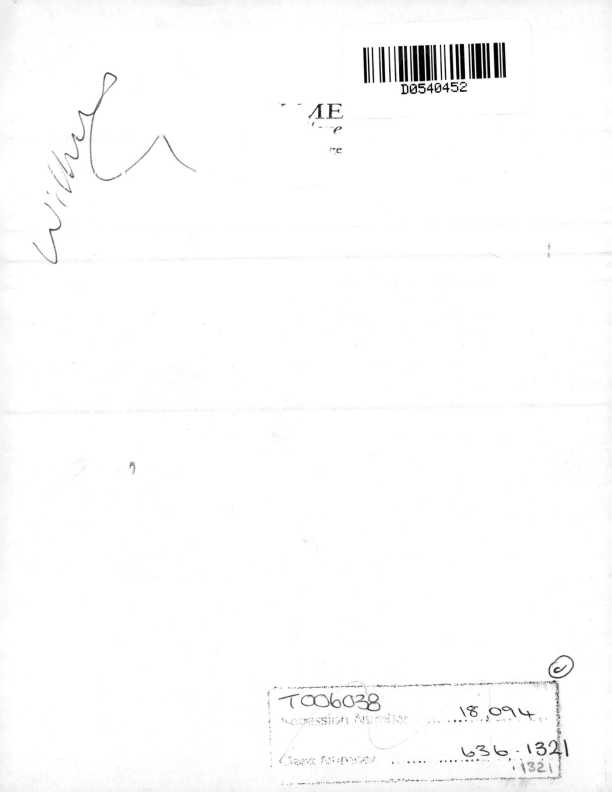

The Reins of Life

'Ready to mount?'

The Reins of Life

An instructional and informative manual
on riding for the disabled

Revised Edition

John Anthony Davies

Foreword by HRH The Princess Royal, GCVO
President of the Riding for the Disabled Association

J. A. ALLEN
London

First published in Great Britain by
J. A. Allen & Co. Ltd
1 Lower Grosvenor Place
London 3W1W 0EL
1967

Second, revised edition published 1988

British Library Cataloguing in Publication Data
Davies, John Anthony
    The reins of life: an instructional and
    informative manual on riding for the disabled.
    ——Rev. ed.
    1. Horsemanship ——— Study and teaching
    2. Physically handicapped ——— Recreation
    I. Title
    798'.2'3'0816   SF310.5

ISBN 0–85131–449–X

Typeset in 12 on 13 point Plantin by
Input Typesetting Ltd, London
Printed and bound in Great Britain by
A. Wheaton and Co. Ltd, Exeter

Contents

This book is dedicated with pride and admiration to all disabled riders who by their courage have made it possible.

I Saw a Child

I saw a child who couldn't walk,
sit on a horse, laugh and talk.
Then ride it through a field of daisies
and yet he could not walk unaided,
I saw a child, no legs below,
sit on a horse, and make it go
through woods of green
and places he had never been
to sit and stare,
except from a chair.

I saw a child who could only crawl
mount a horse and sit up tall.
Put it through degrees of paces
and laugh at the wonder in our faces.
I saw a child born into strife,
take up and hold the reins of life
and that same child was heard to say,
"Thank God for showing me the way . . . "

John Anthony Davies

(Dedicated to Riding for the Disabled International)

Foreword

by HRH The Princess Royal, GCVO
President of the Riding for the Disabled Association

In 1966 the *Reins of Life* was one of the first books published on the subject of teaching horsemanship to the handicapped of all ages. This revised and updated edition has progressed with modern thinking and includes current methods employed by highly qualified instructors and therapists the world over, who daily devote their knowledge and experience to this most modern field of rehabilitation.

John Davies has devoted over thirty years to this movement, both as a Director and Instructor of the Chigwell Centre in England and as Past President of the North American Riding for the Handicapped Association in the United States.

His in-depth knowledge and understanding of the needs of the disabled and the training of the horse for their benefit and enjoyment should be a guide and an inspiration to all.

Anne

Acknowledgments

The author wishes to acknowledge the help given in compiling the original manuscript by the late Dorian Williams, OBE, MFH, Mrs Doreen Allen, MCSP, Dip. TP, and Mrs J. Hughes, MCSP, SRP, physiotherapists to the Riding for the Disabled Trust; the chartered Society of Physiotherapy for permission to use certain photographs; Mrs Norah Jacques, Mr Robert Collishon, the Founding Members, Trustees and staff of the Riding for the Disabled Trust, Chigwell for their support and encouragement.

Sincere thanks must go to HRH The Princess Royal, GCVO, President of the Riding for the Disabled Association, for graciously consenting to provide a foreword for the new edition.

Also in connection with this revised edition the author acknowledges the kind cooperation of the following people and organisations, many of whom supplied photographs free of charge: Keith Webb and the Diamond Riding Centre, *page* 25, 155, 129, 161; Patti Mack, 21, 41, 66–67, 78; Debbie Hall, PRDT, cover illustration; David J. Griffiths, 50; Findlay Kember, 55, 59, 63 (bottom), 153; Brian Folkes, 167 (right); Adrian Hare, 167 (left); Martello Plastics, 63 (top); *Horse & Rider* Magazine, 141, 158; Sport & General, 142; Meldreth Manor; Mr and Mrs Brooks McCormick (United States). The original line drawings are by David C. Bonnett, with additional revised drawings by John Smith.

John Anthony Davies
April, 1988

Introduction

How it All Started

This book has been written for the benefit and information of proprietors of riding schools or similar equestrian establishments, who intend to make facilities available for teaching disabled people to ride, or who may have had requests from parents, doctors or physiotherapists to accept them as students. It is also intended as a guide to instructors who may never have had a disabled person to instruct and may be wondering just how to set about it, and how far their pupil can be expected to progress.

This information is based on the experiences gained by the author teaching the disabled during the last twenty-five years, and in particular while Chief Instructor at the Riding Centre for the Disabled at Grange Farm, Chigwell, Essex, which was the first purpose-built centre of its kind in the world. It was designed with the sole intention of furthering the use of horse riding in the rehabilitation of disabled children and adults. The term 'disabled rider' refers to students who have been or are presently affected by one of the following conditions and who may derive benefits in one form or another from this modern therapeutic recreational activity.

Orthopaedic conditions:
(1) Amputees (varying types)
(2) Scoliosis
(3) Legg Perthes disease (crumbling hip joint)
(4) Arthritis (osteo and rheumatoid)

Neurological diseases:
(1) Poliomyelitis (varying involvement)
(2) Spina bifida

(3) Multiple (disseminated) sclerosis
(4) Cerebral palsy (varying types)
(5) Traumatic paraplegia (spinal cord injuries)
(6) Cerebral vascular accidents (strokes)
(7) Spinal menengitis
(8) Traumatic brain damage (acquired by accident)

Other classifications:
(1) Muscular dystrophy
(2) Autism
(3) Blindness
(4) Hearing and speech impairments
(5) Mental subnormality (varying types)
(6) Epilepsy (varying types)
(7) Learning disabilities
(8) Emotionally disturbed

The original inspiration to use horses in this way was sparked off by the example of Mme Lis Hartel, the world-renowned dressage rider of Denmark, who although severely paralysed by poliomyelitis, insisted on riding again and eventually reached championship form to win a silver medal at the 1952 Helsinki Olympic Games.

Mrs Elsebet Bödthker, a Norwegian physiotherapist and herself an accomplished horsewoman, had met Lis Hartel and noted her physical progress, and in particular the psychological benefits that Mme Hartel derived from riding. In the early 1950s Mrs Bödthker began to teach her own polio patients to ride, utilising both basic equestrian exercises and those used by physiotherapists in clinics. Miss Ulla Harpoth, another physiotherapist from the orthopaedic hospital in Copenhagen, also began to prescribe this activity for her patients.

It soon became apparent, even after only a few months of riding, that children and adolescents disabled by post-poliomyelitis were benefiting in numerous ways from this form of exercise.

News of their progress in riding ability and the physical and psychological improvement soon spread and Mrs Norah Jacques from England, who knew Mrs Bödthker and had provided her with ponies, decided to attempt to establish something more permanent.

After initially using her own ponies in the garden of her house in Essex for post-polio youngsters from St Margaret's hospital, Epping, Mrs Jacques finally managed to obtain the use of the Forest Lodge Riding School in March 1958.

The proprietor of this establishment, Mr Gerry Van der Gucht, himself an amputee, loaned his facility and ponies free, and assisted with the teaching.

Students were also sent from St Thomas's hospital, London, accompanied by their head physiotherapist Miss Doreen Allen, who supervised the mounted exercises.

Increasingly it became obvious that these young students were also benefiting from this form of therapy (for indeed it was now becoming recognised as such) and requests were received from vast numbers of parents with disabled children who wanted to participate.

Doctors and therapists from many hospitals in the Greater London area began to re-evaluate and recommend their patients to take up riding.

At this time, also in the late 1950s, Dr and Mrs Strang of the British Polio Fellowship in South Shields and Miss Stella Saywell, head physical therapist at the Winford Orthopaedic Hospital in Bristol, began teaching their own patients. By 1960 it became obvious to the Jacques that to continue to operate on a part-time basis at a small riding school was no longer practical, so the task of finding somewhere to build a permanent purpose-built riding centre for the disabled was undertaken. However, this was no easy matter and many years went by before a site was found.

The land, given by Sir Donald Allen, comprised nearly four acres. Grange Farm, as it is known, overlooks the Roding Valley on the edge of the green belt in the village of Chigwell, only ten miles from the centre of London.

Donations from the London Parochial Charities, the Sir William Coxen Trust, the Pilgrim Trust, the Ponies of Britain Club, the Chase Charity and the Sembal Trust made the building possible. The Pony Clubs of Britain also collected substantial contributions which helped to equip the facility.

When the Centre was opened in 1964 it was the first purpose-built riding school with a fully qualified staff, both medical and equestrian, and the special facilities, knowledge and equipment necessary for teaching riding as a purposeful therapy and psychologically beneficial form of rehabilitation.

With the opening of the Centre, the Riding for the Disabled Trust, as it was then known, headed by its Patron, the Duchess of Norfolk, became the most authoritative organisation in the world for this type of recreational therapy.

In late 1967 a working party was set up to investigate the possibility of forming a national organisation. Known as the Advisory Council on Riding for the Disabled it consisted of members from the Pony Riding for the Disabled Trust, the British Horse Society, the Pony Club and the Chartered Society of Physiotherapy.

Three years later the Riding for the Disabled Association was formed with the Duchess of Norfolk as its first President. In 1971 HRH The Princess Anne accepted the invitation to become the Patron.

Since those early movements in Scandinavia and England, Riding for the Disabled as a recognised form of progressive therapy and rehabilitation has now become an international organisation. At an international conference in England over four hundred delegates attended, representing twenty different countries.

Other countries with their own national organisations now include the USA, Australia, Canada, New Zealand, Germany, France, Holland, Denmark, Norway, Thailand, and Switzerland. Many other countries, including some behind the Iron Curtain, have begun to institute programmes and form similar organisations. The constant exchange of ideas and experiences between all these associations, is a unique example of international understanding and cooperation for the benefit of mankind and in particular, an understanding of the needs and desires of disabled persons whose afflictions recognise no boundaries.

The explosive growth of this movement, particularly during the last twenty years and the acceptance of its value for certain disabilities, by a once sceptical medical profession, is proof of its need and evidence of its benefits.

No other activity can give the disabled person such a feeling of complete freedom, awareness of self in space and independence of others. No other activity is so psychologically uplifting or so rewarding to everyone concerned.

Since its completion in 1964 the Chigwell Centre has accepted thousands of patients as students and the success stories of riders who were once confined to wheelchairs, or who could not walk without the aid of crutches or sticks, would certainly fill this book. We are not concerned, however, with heart-rending or glowing accounts of individual courage, but with the practical day-to-day methods of instruction and the organising of a riding programme for the disabled.

It must be stressed that this book is written by a riding instructor and explains the basic methods for teaching the disabled to actually ride a horse by their own ability. It should be noted and emphasised that any specific difficulties experienced by the disabled rider and the complexities of each individual disability, should be discussed fully with the therapist at the initial assessment before lessons commence, and at each upgrading or advancing stage in the individual's tuition.

Full cooperation between the instructor and therapist is essential. Indeed, each will benefit greatly by studying the other's profession very closely.

Riding is a recreational, therapeutic activity, that brings to the disabled a wealth of benefits not experienced by participation in more conventional or more readily available forms of recreational activity. It is still, however, in its infancy and we are continually learning and discovering just how much benefit the disabled derive from the sport. The pleasurable experience, the association and the companionship, along with the delights of independence, are, without doubt, obvious. If only for these reasons the disabled should be encouraged to participate whenever and wherever possible.

1 Methods of Instruction

The person with perhaps the greatest burden of responsibility in this whole scheme is the instructor: he is the one in closest contact, on him everyone relies, and for him everyone concerned in the programme contributes. This is not a burden to be borne lightly, and great sacrifices will be expected both mentally and physically. To the disabled rider the instructor is perhaps the one person who gives hope for a brighter future, so the teacher must never underestimate the task before him.

Before a pupil is accepted it is essential that contact be made with the student's doctor, hospital and therapist, to obtain full medical approval and history. These experts and the parents should be consulted regarding the exact type and degree of disability and the limitations that may be imposed upon the student as a result. The therapist in particular must be consulted at the initial evaluation session with regard to the type and extent of exercises to be included in the riding lessons. Great damage can be caused if a pupil is made to perform exercises that are not approved or of which the student may not be capable. (See chapter on exercises.) Pinned joints or those fixed by orthopaedic surgery are an obvious reason for this precaution.

The student's mental ability must also be taken into consideration so that the instructor can plan the kind of attitude or approach to adopt when instructing. Simply because the rider is physically disabled the instructor should not presume mental incompetency. A disciplined approach combined with an appreciation of the capabilities and needs of the rider will produce the best results. The instructor must be able to control his emotions, particularly the one of frustration which will often be experienced when trying to obtain perfection. He should learn to be satisfied with even small steps in progress and encourage the rider by whatever means to even greater exertion and self-help.

This feeling of frustration also occurs a great deal in disabled students, especially when, because of their disability, they experience difficulty in accomplishing a certain task, despite being mentally aware of how it should be done. For this reason it is obvious that the teacher should never make his own emotions apparent, as this would only tend to discourage the student even more.

Physically the rider will progress at a much slower rate than he will psychologically. Almost the first time a disabled rider is mounted he receives an enormous psychological boost to his morale and well-being, when he suddenly becomes aware of his ability to utilise the four strong legs of the horse to his own advantage.

Suddenly being hoisted into the air and put into the unaccustomed position of looking down on people, probably for the first time, is tremendously psychologically uplifting. However, with young children the process of mounting for the first time can be a frightening experience so it must be done slowly and with frequent reassurance. (See chapter on mounting.)

The instructor can utilise this psychological realisation on the part of the rider by further encouraging and convincing him that he is capable of even greater physical and mental effort. Bringing the student up to his fullest possible maximum potential is the instructor's primary concern.

Instructors are aware that a great deal of their teaching is by repetition, and it can happen, because of constantly having to repeat lessons, that the instructor gets bored and consequently stale. With the disabled rider the position is made worse by the fact that exercises, for instance, have to be done on practically every lesson, from beginners through to more advanced pupils. The instructor must therefore be inventive and endeavour to vary the type and sequence of exercises and lesson plan and yet still ensure they remain interesting and beneficial to the riders. Boredom must be avoided at all costs. A bored student will not function properly.

If the instructor has a capable qualified assistant who can relieve him for certain well-tested rides, then it will be easier to keep the lessons fresh and interesting both for himself and his students.

Before lessons commence the instructor should determine what his lesson plan will be. This will, of course, vary according to the disabilities and ages of his students. However, the plan should be adhered to as closely as possible and all movements should be progressively more difficult to accomplish. (See chapter on control of a class.)

Immediate results should not be expected and will not be forthcoming except in very isolated cases. Physical improvement, balance, posture and coordination progress slowly, but psychologically there will be a sudden upward surge.

Most disabled pupils have an intense desire to learn, they enjoy every minute on horseback and have the utmost patience. Because of the incentive they work much harder and for much longer periods.

The instructor should be ready to praise even the slightest improvement and encourage the rider by all means to attempt even greater difficulties, within the bounds of safety.

An essential quality is the ability to recognise when a student is not truly capable of response or performance and when he is just lazy or disobedient. The initial assessment or evaluation of the student's ability to ride, is the time for the instructor to also evaluate or determine the student's character, so that he can work out the individual approach that is so essential in the class lesson and fully understand the nature of the person as well as the disability.

The majority of disabled persons understand fully the

reasons why they are being taught to ride, so the instructor should never be too embarrassed to discuss any problems relating to his students as they arise.

In the case of children or riders also suffering from a mental disability, frequent discussion with the therapist, teacher or, in many cases, the parent, can be beneficial in promoting progression.

The instructor should not try to set himself up as a kind of 'equine therapist', but should concentrate instead on what he knows and teach the basics of good horsemanship.

It must be recognised by all those concerned that the therapeutic benefits are obtained as a direct result of the student attempting to 'ride' (i.e. control and influence) the horse by his own physical and mental efforts. The horse itself becomes the therapist through its warmth, movement and constantly changing patterns of rhythm and equilibrium.

Today the term 'hippotherapy' is used by therapists to describe this effect on their patients, who benefit without actually being taught the functional method of riding, and may never in fact ever be capable of doing so. When teaching horsemanship, however, it is the instructor that is the guiding hand, controlling, encouraging and determining the next logical step to be taken.

Therapists are the link between the instructor, the volunteer helpers and the students. They are trained to understand the muscles, joints, tendons and ligaments and everything that makes the body function correctly. They recognise and know how to treat the different disabilities and can see when something is wrong and how to correct it. They are concerned with improvement in the student's ability.

The therapist knows what difficulties the disabled rider will experience when the latter starts to ride and can relate this information to the instructor and the helpers, thereby assisting them in their job of teaching the student horsemanship. When medical consent has been received for a patient to ride, the therapist and instructor together, at the initial

How proud!

assessment and at regular intervals, determine the student's
ability to progress and evaluate a planned programme with
progressive exercises of the right kind.

It is a double safeguard if the student is also evaluated by
the therapist when being mounted, because if for some
reason the pupil is not considered suitable, the problem can
be referred back to the doctor. Basically, however, having
been sent on a doctor's approval the patient will ride.

Some contrary indications which may influence the
decision to accept a student are: lack of sensation in the
lower limbs, pressure sores, epilepsy (unless controlled by
drugs) and incontinency.

When riding for the disabled first began, the more obvious
the handicap, the more it was thought the person should
ride, so that the benefits could be proved. However, it is
no longer necessary to prove them. The instructor's first
concern must be whether the student is manageable on a
horse and is it safe? He must ask the question: is this student
capable of maintaining a reasonable balance and controlling
the horse, eventually by his own efforts, in spite of the
limitations imposed by the disability?

With the cooperation of the therapist, who should attend
regularly (if not all sessions), the instructor will soon become
experienced in observing and recognising what is wrong and
how it can be corrected or compensated for.

If the student is never going to be capable of applying an
aid or performing a movement in the normally accepted
way, then another method must be found to accomplish the
same end by compensation. This can be done by utilising a
different part of the body to compensate for any area of
weakness. It must not be done by gimmicks or special equipment, designed to make it easier for the rider to accomplish
the task.

The instructor must realise before starting to teach the
disabled, that the student will seldom, if ever, become a
really proficient rider. There are not many Lis Hartels.

It must be recognised that riding, or any other form of

therapy, is never going to make a student normal again. The best that can be hoped for is noticeable improvement in ability, and one should strive towards normality by encouraging the student towards maximum self-help that is so necessary to obtain maximum benefit.

Horses and some domesticated animals, it has been stated, respond to thought waves, or 'thought transference' as it is sometimes called, so the instructor might do well to concentrate on the mind of the rider in the first instance. If he can convince his pupil that he is mentally and physically capable of controlling the horse, then the rider will in turn find less difficulty in transferring his thoughts and 'aids' to his horse with less physical effort and strain. The physical development and improvement will follow a natural course from sound psychological foundations.

Slowly the benefits will become obvious and as the student progresses a small step at a time, the delight, the sheer joy on the face of the pupil makes the whole frustrating, long-drawn-out process worthwhile.

The instructor must exercise extreme patience, yet remain firm; he must be humorous but not sarcastic, strong-willed but not overbearing; then perhaps he will obtain results. He is there to help the students attain their aims by calculated, progressive lessons in a controlled class situation which requires a special knowledge and discipline.

The sequence of lessons remains the same as for all beginner groups. Introduction, mounting, position, dismount, the aids, the halt, the walk, etc., but for many reasons the time spent on any one will vary greatly between individuals. Standard acceptable aids that are normally used may have to be adapted, refined, or even completely altered to obtain a response.

An instructor who is not in control of the class and is not aware of the progressive stages of teaching will not only have chaos, frustration and confusion in the lesson and produce poor equestrians, but also is a distinct threat to everyone's safety.

2 Control of a Class

Regardless of whether the disability is an orthopaedic condition or some form of mental disorder, the basic class methods of instruction that apply to any student learning to ride a horse remain the same.

It is imperative for safety, for clarification, and for normal progression that acceptable rules concerning control of a class are studied and applied, if students are to receive the maximum knowledge and benefit. This is particularly important with disabled riders, because of the increased number of persons who may be required to attend the lesson. Volunteers, leaders, side helpers, and the therapist are examples. The greater the numbers involved, the higher the safety risk factor and the more difficulty there is in controlling and teaching.

The following basic guidelines are the same as those taught and followed by responsible associations and equestrian establishments throughout the western world, in particular, those who train instructors. They are based on experience and sound common sense.

Even before lessons actually begin, there are a number of factors to be considered that may affect the instructor's methods of approach and ultimate control and response. At the initial introduction and student evaluation, riders should be graded into a similar standard of expertise and knowledge. With non-handicapped students, the instructor would determine the level of riding skills by giving a short trial lesson and discussing previous riding experience. Oral, as well as physical, tests must be given to the handicapped student to determine the full extent of 'know how' even though difficulties may be experienced in the actual performance. Once a standard is established the student should be placed in a class of the same, or slightly higher, level to encourage competitive progression.

With a disabled student, the instructor is obviously not only concerned with the equestrian ability, but also he must fully understand the degree and type of disability. The evaluation must therefore include grading into a class where fellow students are, as far as possible, similarly handicapped, not only with regard to the type of disability but also the degree of involvement. This will ensure the rider does not feel put down or left out in any way.

For the preservation of self-esteem and confidence, it is not recommended that both physical and mental disabilities are taught in the same class, nor even adults with children unless necessary or unavoidable due to circumstances.

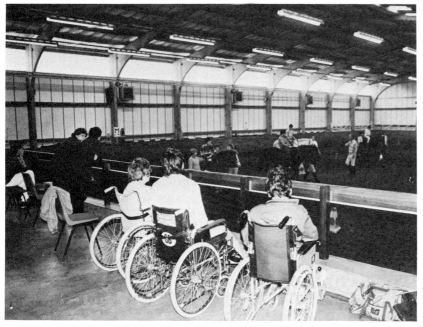

Waiting riders watch keenly from the viewing gallery.

This evaluation from the instructor's point of view is, of course, to determine what difficulties, other than the normal ones, will have to be overcome before the student can become an independent rider. The ability of the student is therefore the instructor's primary concern.

The therapist, however, is more concerned with the benefits the student may derive from the effort involved in attempting to ride and become an independent rider. The disability is therefore the therapists' concern.

This dual evaluation and continuing cooperation between instructor and therapist forms the basis for a long term overall plan to make it possible for the student to eventually become capable of controlling the horse by his own individual effort, while receiving the maximum benefit.

The student's character, behaviour, and overall attitude toward the idea of riding should also be a major consideration before lessons are undertaken.

Safety is the first consideration in all classes and it is the sole responsibility of the instructor to make a final check on all equipment before the lesson begins, including saddles, bridles, special equipment and any items used for games, jumping or exercises. Other equipment not required immediately or not in use, should be put in a safe place where it will not interfere with the progression of the lesson, or constitute a danger to the horses or a distraction to the students.

An example of the need for this personal visual and physical check by the instructor is where stirrups may need to be purposely at odd lengths for a specific disability (e.g. a hemiplegic or an amputee with a false limb).

Onlookers, such as parents, volunteers, or observers, should be requested to remain in one place if they have to stay and should not be allowed to talk or participate in any way in the lesson unless directed to do so by the instructor. Parents have an inherent desire to communicate with their children during lessons. This must be deterred and other children watching must be kept under control.

If parents have to stay during classes, it is desirable to occupy them in some way. The same applies to brothers, sisters, cousins, aunts, and, in particular, grandparents.

Obviously, a special 'open day' can be arranged annually for students to demonstrate their riding skills before an invited audience, which can include all of those people. After a full term of riding, the benefits are far more noticeable than at each weekly session and students delight in showing how much progress they have made. The extra efforts put into a 'parents' day' demonstration by the riders, makes it well worth the work involved in putting it on.

The number of students in any class will obviously reflect on the standard of tuition and the amount of benefit derived. The arena, as previously mentioned, can become a little overcrowded with leaders and side helpers participating, so the smaller the class, the better. Four, or a maximum of six, in a class is ideal for control. As riders progress and helpers are withdrawn to another group, the numbers can be increased. By this time faster gaits are employed and lessons can include ground pole work and some elementary jumping.

Handicapped riders also require far more individual attention in the early stages and this is not possible with a larger class.

The working area to be used for lessons should be carefully selected and will depend on the climate, available land and financial resources. Ideally, an enclosed or indoor arena is preferred, but if not actually enclosed, a solid well-made fenced arena is necessary.

Rails should be on the inside of posts to avoid wrenched feet or bruised knees. Completely closed sides that slope out at the bottom, keep the horses off the rails and prevent helpers on the outside from being pitched against the boards.

Gates or doors should open outwards, slide behind the wall, or lift up.

The type of surface is a matter of personal choice and

depends on a number of factors, including the instructor's preference and experience, the state of the local soil and the cost. However, it should certainly be well drained, workable, and resilient. Indoor surfaces can consist of peat moss, tan bark, or wood shavings, or any combination of the above, on a base of clay or crushed limestone screenings. Clay, however, alone does tend to become shiny and slippery, allowing the upper layers to move, whereas limestone screenings grip the surface covering better. Whatever the choice, it should be kept damped down by spraying with water or light oil to prevent dust and regularly raked to prevent banking.

Outside manèges should be properly excavated and constructed to facilitate good drainage and finished off again with limestone screenings which do stay in place when damped and a final surface of a maximum three inches of sharp sand. Some schools prefer deeper sand for working horses, but this is a matter of opinion.

Horse droppings should be removed to lessen the risk of infection, particularly tetanus. It should be remembered that the handicapped student, who often leads a more sheltered life than the average person, is more susceptible to infections.

Whatever the type of material used, it should be able to stand up to regular pounding and be 'soft on landing' in the event of tumbles, which are the least pleasant but most inevitable part of learning to ride.

Leaders and side helpers, as well as the ponies, find that deep surfaces can be heavy-going and very tiring to the calf muscles.

If the lessons are given on a grassy area, the mounts should be fitted with overhead check reins which will prevent a pony from suddenly lowering its head to graze. This habit, if it becomes so, will invariably pull the rider off balance.

An average sized arena of 70ft x 140ft or larger, can be divided in half temporarily so that the instructor can stay in closer contact with the students until they dispense with volunteer leaders and can proceed unassisted at the faster paces. The temporary fencing or hurdles used to divide the arena should extend across the complete width without any gaps, and should be painted white to increase visibility. Horses and riders should be familiarised with the partition before the lessons commence, to prevent shying and accidents.

The Lesson Plan

Obviously, it is not always possible to adhere to a rigid pre-arranged lesson plan, because invariably, something happens or catches the attention of the instructor that will cause the plan to be changed or abandoned. However, a progressive routine and a distinctive method of teaching are essential, together with an outline plan for particular groups that will cover a full term of riding.

A period of one full hour should be allowed and is usually sufficient to cover reception, mounting, and the lesson. The dismounting may or may not be included, depending on the standard of expertise and the assistance required. As students become more expert at mounting and dismounting, they will receive longer periods in the saddle and consequently more benefit.

The specific subject taught in the lesson will naturally depend on the standard of the class and the extent of the individual disabilities. However, all classes should include a warming up or relaxing period, an equestrian subject (first trotting lesson, the canter, etc.), exercises agreed beforehand with the therapist, and with children, perhaps a mounted game or competition.

Adult 'games' can be more purposeful and can include elementary dressage movements and ground pole work leading to jumping.

All lessons should follow, as closely as possible, the principles of good horsemanship and acceptable standards of instruction. Students must constantly be tested to the ultimate level of their potential If they are to receive the maximum benefit.

The warming-up period should be used by the instructor not only to relax the riders and get them 'down in the saddle' but also for observing very carefully the exact nature of the individual problem and determine what corrections, if any, in posture, balance, or coordination may be necessary.

During this warm-up period, lessons from previous classes can be reviewed. Provided there are no problems and the movements are accomplished reasonably well, the class can then begin to progress to another stage. This is where the planning of progressive lessons is so important.

The instructor, however, must be flexible and ready to adapt the plan very quickly to immediate and individual requirements; bearing in mind that some students will naturally regress initially for the first few lessons or at the commencement of others.

The disabled rider must be evaluated on the horse in the same manner as a non-handicapped student. Position of the body, head, legs and hands, balance and recovery, coordination, and application of the aids must all be observed, recorded, and corrected. In this respect, there is no difference at all between the two groups. Knowing what the correct picture of a rider should be and applying this to all students, is the basic principle of teaching horsemanship. The actual disability merely becomes another hurdle for the instructor and student to overcome or compensate for, in what may become unique and individual ways.

Regardless of the level of expertise or individual problems, the basic lesson plan remains the same and is as follows:

Explanation. Explanations should be brief and to the point, describing the specific lesson to be taught. Lengthy explanations should be avoided as they tend to bore the class.

Demonstration. In a class of handicapped riders, the

instructor will probably not be mounted. If a mounted demonstration is required, it can be advantageous and psychologically beneficial to use one of the students for the demonstration. 'Seeing is believing' and in a class where riders are similarly handicapped, a demonstration by one of the group avoids frustration and encourages greater effort. Even blind students can be made to 'see' with their hands and feel position and the application of the aids physically by touching. 'A picture is worth a thousand words.'

Interrogation. Before the class begins to try out a new movement, the students must be questioned briefly to determine whether or not the explanation has been fully understood. This, of course, can take longer with some individuals than with others. The learning disabled and the mentally retarded will require a simpler explanation and a more graphic demonstration with a deeper interrogation than students with a physical handicap, who may, in turn, find more of a problem in the actual performance of a movement.

Imitation and Repetition. These are the final learning stages where the class attempts to imitate the instructor or the picture that was created. Children, in particular, are wonderful imitators, and this fact can be used to good advantage. Repetition is, of course, necessary for advancement, with repeated corrections to attain improvement, benefit, and hopefully, perfection.

The attitude or manner of the instructor is probably the most important single factor in influencing and controlling the class. As previously stated, if the instructor's attitude tends to be soft or pitying, or in any way condescending, the class will react in a negative manner. On the other hand, an overforceful, bullying or sarcastic attitude will cause a retardation of interest and eventual withdrawal.

The instructor should, of course, be knowledgeable, kindly yet persuasive, and able to instil a sense of confidence and a desire on the part of the rider to please. There must be a determination to see the riders improve, combined with

A class lesson in progress

an appreciation of the multiple personal requirements and difficulties that each student experiences. Discipline must be combined with endless patience, boundless energy and inventiveness. Above all, the instructor must possess a sense of humour and the ability to communicate or relate to the students, so that the lesson becomes a pleasurable experience and the fun that riding should be if the benefits are to be derived.

The appearance or mode of dress of the instructor is a very important aspect and part of an overall picture that can create a favourable or poor impression. It is obvious that an instructor correctly attired in riding wear, will instil a much stronger sense of trust and admiration and will consequently encourage a greater effort from the student to imitate.

In my experience, I have never had any reason to believe that students resent the instructor who dresses correctly. In fact, I would say that more casual attire could lead to a careless response, which may be of benefit to some hyperactive riders, but could mean a less persuasive impulse for the majority.

Classes taken by correctly attired instructors have always responded to the more authoritative appearance. The desire to imitate and be correct, as in any sport, has proven very beneficial psychologically to both students and volunteers!

It is recognised, of course, that many handicapped students will experience certain difficulties in obtaining or even affording the correct attire. This stumbling block may be overcome by allowing the riders to be somewhat less formal at certain times.

The fitting of boots and breeches for some physical disabilities may also present difficulties which can cause allowances to be made. Amputees and persons who have to wear leg braces or callipers are two examples.

The extra time taken to dress and prepare for each lesson should also be considered.

Safety and comfort must not be put at risk by allowing loose-fitting jeans that may cause rubbing or pressure sores. Shoes that do not give protection to the front of the ankle, where the stirrup comes into contact, such as plimsoles or sneakers, should also be discouraged. Whatever the attire of both instructor and student, neatness, safety and serviceability should be the final guidelines.

The instructors' voice can create a good or poor impression, in the same way as does appearance and dress. The tone of voice reflects the instructor's attitude or mood and will affect the students' subsequent response. A firm, clear voice of normal mid-pitch, without any hint of doubt or panic, will instil trust and confidence within the rider.

Experienced instructors know how to project themselves and their voice without shouting or raising the pitch to a hysterical note, which will not only put the students on edge but can also cause even the most docile of animals to fidget. The more highly bred the animal, the more likely it is to react suddenly to a higher pitch.

Horses that have been trained to respond obediently to the instructor's voice on the lunge, for example, can be a help in the beginning stages, but it should be recognised that they can also react violently without warning at the wrong moment and perhaps un-nerve or even unseat a student. Alternatively, a dull, monotonous tone will bring a similarly lethargic response.

When addressing a stationary class, commands and explanations should be given by the instructor facing the group, preferably with a solid wall or fence behind them to reflect the sound.

Very clear and precise commands ought to be given in simple equestrian vocabulary until the student understands the more descriptive terms. Technical phrases should be minimised to avoid confusion and explanations kept short and unhurried to ensure complete understanding. The class should be interrogated following explanations to be certain of comprehension before attempting any new movement.

When the class is on the move, commands must be kept brief and to the point, given directly to the individual student at fault using his or her name as a prefix. Even though the handicapped rider may not be totally aware, personal names should always be used when making direct individual corrections.

Terminology and vocabulary must be kept fresh, avoiding stock phrases such as 'OK?', 'Alright?', 'There you go!', 'That's great!', etc. Originality is the keynote and self-criticism is a valuable asset for the instructor.

A periodic tape recording of a lesson is a great help in making instructors aware of their own failings. Video equipment is of course invaluable for both students and instructor for evaluation and progression.

Most horses that are used in regular classes soon learn to recognise and understand the instructor's voice and even anticipate certain phrases and commands; particularly 'Walk on,' 'Halt,' and 'Canter'. This can be used to the instructor's advantage in the early stages of learning, but later it may be necessary to change the type of command for certain movements, to avoid sudden transitions which take the rider unawares and could cause a loss of balance and a threat to safety. Substitution of numbers for words for certain movements is one way of avoiding this problem.

The instructor must set the tone of his commands according to the class. A lethargic, less-responsive group will require a brisk, sharper tone; whereas with a more hyperactive group, quieter, softer tones are more effective.

Another important aspect in the control of a class is positioning. The instructor, the volunteers, and the horses must be positioned correctly at varying times and for various reasons throughout the lesson.

Instructors who insist on following each and every individual student all around the arena at every pace, are unfortunately an all-too-common sight. Corrections have to be given in short, jerky gasps as they run alongside, eventually almost tripping over their own feet in their desire to keep up. These are the ones who complain of being tired after only two hours' teaching. They deserve to work in an office! It would be better if instructors were made to take a class with their feet tied together. It is not necessary to run after each rider. Not only is it physically exhausting but it is also very distracting to the student being followed, while the rest of the class stand and are ignored.

The simple practice of walking a few steps diagonally each way from the centre of the arena, similar to the method of loose schooling a young horse, will enable the instructor to observe the whole ride at a glance. Corrections can then be made verbally by controlled voice projection and by using volunteer side helpers as a physical extension of the instructor and to aid reinforcement. The use of side helpers in positioning the rider and physically correcting the aids is of tremendous help to the instructor and student alike.

For stationary explanations, and particularly in the exercise period, the class should be halted and lined up facing the instructor, preferably on the short side of the arena, with the length of the arena in front in case a mounted demonstration is necessary. If the class is full with leaders and side helpers, then the class can be positioned on the long side, but this does restrict the space available for mounted demonstrations which should be seen by the class to the front.

The most logical place for the instructor to stand so that the whole class can see and hear, is in the centre and far enough back to be able to take in the whole ride at a glance. Standing too close to the group, or to an individual, will restrict vision for everyone. A good rule is that whatever the length of the ride, the instructor should stand an equal distance from them, as on a triangle. The larger the ride, the further back one should stand.

There is sometimes a tendency for instructors to become mesmerised by a certain rider and to gradually move in towards the centre student. This should be avoided, because it will mean that riders at the extreme ends may have to crane forward to hear or see, while the individual in the centre begins to get a guilt complex. Eventually, for either reason, the class will lose interest and concentration and consequently fail to derive knowledge and benefit.

The positioning of horses on the move or stationary is also a safety consideration. On the rail, going around the outside of the arena, an equal distance or one horse's length should be maintained to avoid clashes. Even the best behaved horses can resent having their rear ends used as buffers.

Should a rider have to pull up for any reason when not directed to do so, the whole ride should also halt smoothly. This is particularly important with beginners and students who may require side helpers to assist with balance recovery.

Overtaking close to another horse can create problems and the habit of circling away suddenly can take the rider by surprise. Advanced students who ride independently, without the need of helpers, may of course circle away or halt at will.

There are times when it is advantageous to open the ride out to greater distances, when using the whole arena, to give the student a greater responsibility in controlling the horse.

If the ride continues to stay in the closed file position for any length of time, it can become a habit with the animals and aggravate their natural herding instincts which will develop into troublesome 'napping' tendencies.

When halted for explanations, demonstrations, and exercises in particular, the correct spacing between horses must be observed. In this regard, leaders and side helpers should not only be briefed on how to lead, but also on how to assist the rider to maintain equal distance at all times. The freedom of natural movement of the horse, however, should be interfered with as little as possible.

Dressage letters equally spaced around the arena are extremely useful for designating position and spacing, as well as their normal function for equestrian movements and transitions. They are also of immense value in games and exercises for certain disabilities, where the testing of speech and vocabulary may be required.

To avoid mishaps, instructors and volunteers should always be on the lookout for obvious warning signs, both from the horse and rider. Leaders, in particular, should watch the horses' ears to see how they react in certain situations. Also, the eyes will show white when the horse is frightened or uncomfortable. However, some horses, such as Appaloosas, naturally show white eyes. The tail will lift when the horse is aggravated or annoyed, and swishing, other than for insects, usually precedes a kick.

Similar obvious signs also occur in the rider, be it for different reasons, and volunteers and instructors should be capable of recognising them and acting upon instinct. Fear and frustration are apparent, as is disobedience and behavioural problems which should be handled in the same way as in any normal class. Consultation with the special teacher or therapist at the initial evaluation will determine any special approach.

Frustration is probably the most difficult hurdle for the handicapped student and the instructor to overcome. In particular, possessing the knowledge of how to accomplish a movement or exercise, but being physically incapable of completing it, is often more of a severe set-back than, perhaps, not being mentally aware.

It can be overcome, however, by compensation and inventiveness by the instructor and within the individual student. Praise for the smallest achievement, patience, and perseverance will help to alleviate this problem. The use of competitive games to encourage advancement and making much of what can be accomplished will also lessen the feeling.

Fatigue and subsequent lack of concentration are not so obvious. Over-tired students will quickly lose coordination and balance, which in turn becomes a serious risk factor and a threat to safety. The tell-tale signs are there, and should be watched for: sleepiness, dropped eyelids, rocking motions, fidgeting, and irritability are some of the more obvious symptoms.

The length of time the disabled student can endure the demands of riding in a class situation, which is physically and mentally more demanding than riding out alone, will depend on the degree and type of disability, the student's age and previous experience. These will all obviously vary greatly between individuals in the same class and the method of coping with them in a group of disabled riders is a great deal more difficult and demanding than with a non-handicapped class, who can take a full hour of concentrated work without too much effort.

The instructor should always endeavour to experience the same difficulty the rider has by imitating and adopting a similar position or fault. This method can be used both for correcting position and improving the aids of the rider who has difficulty in controlling the horse. It will also enable a decision to be made regarding the use of any special equipment that can help overcome the problem of rider frustration.

Physically and mentally the instructor should 'ride' each horse and then transfer or impart his conclusions to the student. By this method an instinct or feel for the horse will be instilled in the rider that will eventually develop into his own personal understanding and hopefully will become second nature. After a few sessions, the instructor will notice that corrections do not have to be made quite so often, as the students begin to react and correct themselves.

Riders should be encouraged by every means to help themselves, and even small achievements should be praised to increase the incentive. However, miracles are rare and sudden surges forward should not be expected. Success and improvement are measured in very small doses and it takes the utmost concentration and cooperation to achieve them.

Horseback riding for the disabled, as for most students, is considered a 'risk exercise' with a certain element of danger, which can stimulate the rider to greater effort that will eventually bring benefits which other less active sports do not. All exercise increases awareness and subsequent physical and mental reactions. The infusion of a little fear, properly controlled, will enhance the result and not only improve functional activities, but will also carry over into other activities of daily living. With knowledge and experience in good class control, the instructor can be almost certain that the risk of riding will be of benefit to the rider and not a threat to safety.

It should be remembered that as with all learning experiences, the student must enjoy it to derive benefit. The instructor who forgets that riding should be enjoyable and fun, will soon lose control of the class.

3 The Leaders

At any establishment that intends to teach disabled students, it must be recognised that volunteer helpers and leaders are essential, not only for beginners but also for the more advanced riders, to assist in mounting procedures and to hold horses during the stationary exercise periods.

In many riding schools there are often groups of people who act as leaders for small children and nervous adult first-timers in the early stages of learning to ride. Unfortunately, it is very often a case of parents, bystanders or even young inexperienced children, being pressed into helping out at the last minute, in spite of the fact that they may be frightened of horses and regardless of their 'horse sense'. Very seldom are definite arrangements made to ensure that a knowledgeable or responsible person is in charge of each horse, or indeed in charge of the volunteers!

With disabled riders, who are so dependent on help at first, it is essential that the instructor or organiser of the programme enlists the help of a number of dedicated people and organises them into a group responsible for leading or assisting at the side of the horse or pony. For his own peace of mind, the instructor should make certain that volunteers are taught and understand the correct procedure for leading and assisting with both horse and riders. Classes must also be arranged to train them in the acceptable and safe methods for dealing with the disabled, before they are allowed to assist in an actual class lesson.

At the Chigwell Centre we were fortunate enough to have a group of teenage riders and ladies who lived locally, who formed themselves into a club known as the 'Friends of Disabled Riders'. These volunteers assisted at the Centre in many ways other than leading in the arena, including help in the reception area, mounting, transportation, fund-raising and public relations. The ladies also provided refreshments after lessons and at special events such as open days.

Other volunteers who were active in the administration of the programme were a physical therapist, a doctor, a lawyer, an accountant and a secretary.

Whether or not such a club is formed, a coordinator must be appointed who is responsible for recruiting sufficient volunteers for each class and notifying them of any changes in times or routine. Recruitment should be undertaken seriously and early enough for training to be completed before classes commence. Approaches can be made personally by lecture visits, mail or through publicity and advertising. Demonstrations to the public at horse shows and events always creates an interest and invariably brings a response to appeals for help.

An escorted hack can be enjoyable for all.

Other sources of potential volunteers include local riding stables, hunts, pony clubs and similar horse organisations. Outside of the equine world contacts can be made with organisations such as Rotary, Inner Wheel, churches, youth organisations (cadets, scouts and guides), schools and colleges.

It is recommended that the minimum responsible age for a volunteer to lead or help in the lesson is fourteen. It should also be remembered that leading or walking alongside a horse or pony for the duration of a lesson can be very exhausting, particularly if the lesson includes a great deal of trotting. Therefore consideration should be given to the fitness and the age of volunteers.

Persons who cannot physically stand the strain of assisting on foot, can be used in another capacity elsewhere within the administration.

Once those required to assist in the lesson or mounting have been chosen, they should attend the briefing and training session, to acquaint them fully with their responsibilities and the instructor's individual methods of teaching and controlling a class.

The volunteers must be taught to realise from the very beginning, that regardless of how much knowledge they already may have about riding, they must respect the instructor's commands and methods at all times. These methods may often differ drastically from the normally accepted methods of instruction or means of attaining a degree of horsemanship from the able-bodied student, and this must be fully understood.

For this reason and to avoid embarrassing situations, volunteer leaders and helpers should also be advised regarding the type and range of the disabilities they will be working with, and the extent to which the individual student is disabled. With this information they can more fully appreciate the degree of difficulty that may be experienced by the rider, and just how much assistance may be required at each new stage.

How to Lead a Horse and Assist the Rider

The term 'to lead a pony' gives the impression to anyone not familiar with horses that the leader has to walk in front to show the way. In fact some leaders, even after training, have this tendency. This is incorrect and dangerous because they cannot see what the pony is up to nor whether the rider is even on board. Sometimes the leader needs to hold the pony back, if it is going too fast, or urge the mount forwards in conjunction with the rider, if it is being lazy.

The main task of the leader is to control the horse in an emergency and to assist the rider in every way possible without actually taking the rider's place. The safety and independence of the rider must always be borne in mind.

Whatever the pace, when leading a pony that is being ridden or not, the leader must always walk level with the shoulder, keeping the pony's head in front. The ears and eyes display warning signals that should always be observed.

The leading rein, whether it is attached to the back of the noseband or the rings of the bit (if it is divided), should never be used to pull the pony forward, rather the animal should be urged forward by the hand pressing against the lower branches of the jawbone into the curb or chin groove, and only then when the pony is obviously disobeying the rider's aids or the rider is not able to use the legs sufficiently to make the animal walk forwards.

Care must be taken to ensure that the pony's head is not merely pushed up in the air (pointing) as this would only tend to pull the rider's arms and body too far forward or cause the reins to slip from grasp. If the leader insists on walking in front, or holds the leading rein directly in front of the pony's mouth, there is a risk of receiving a nasty nip on the forearm or fingers, so for safety's sake the hand should be kept well back.

It must be emphasised that no matter how lazy the pony is, the leader must never try to take the rider's place, either by pulling the pony forward, or turning, or stopping the pony for the rider. Students must always be encouraged to 'ride' the pony alone and by their own ability. The only exception to this rule is when on the first few lessons the instructor is teaching the rider to feel the movement of the pony and obtain a secure 'seat'. At this time the leader will be asked to keep the pony moving forward so that the rider does not have to worry about creating impulsion.

The leaders and helpers can assist the instructor and rider by continually showing the pupil what is meant by the various commands, such as where to apply the leg aids and how to maintain contact through the reins, without becoming dependent upon them for support. Leaders must also try to keep the pony as calm as possible and at a *normal regular pace* and a correct distance from the horse in front, which is approximately 9 feet or one horse's length. A regular rhythmic pace is necessary not only for the rider to feel and learn the paces but also for the rider's body to benefit from the movement and warm, massaging effect to the muscles and joints.

In order that the rider has complete freedom to use the reins correctly, care should be taken to ensure that the leading rein does not run over the top of the rein on the near side, which would tend to put pressure on that rein causing the pony to lean or turn in that direction, without the rider actually wanting to. The leading rein should there-fore run between and under the rider's reins and be held in the hand about 2 inches back, with the other hand taking up the slack in loops. By this method the rider's feel or contact with the pony's mouth is not interfered with.

When a change of direction is required, the leader changes hands by crossing in front of the pony to the opposite side without interfering with the pace. Once the leader has changed sides, the helper at the side can, if necessary, also change by crossing behind.

In an outdoor manège or indoor arena the leader should always lead on the inside rein, keeping the pony between themselves and the wall or fence. They must also remember, of course, that they may have a helper on the off-side of the pony who will object violently and become very ineffective when squashed against the wall.

Cooperation and communication between the leaders and helpers is therefore essential for the safety of all concerned.

At the Halt

One of the most important tasks the leader has to perform, particularly for disabled riders, is when the ride is lined up for the exercise period which forms a part of each lesson. At this time, especially if it is a rather chilly day, the ponies tend to be a little restless and may want to communicate with each other. The leader should stand in front of the pony, holding the lead line but facing the rider.

For exercises the instructor should have the undivided attention of the riders but the horses have probably heard it all before (and don't much care for it anyway) so it is up to the leaders to keep the ponies' attention occupied the best way they can. There are various ways of doing this.

First of all, never hold the pony rigidly tight so that the unfortunate animal cannot even turn or relax his neck. The exercise period occurs after the ponies have been working for some time, so let them rest and look around a little. Providing the class is lined up correctly the risk of ponies kicking or biting their neighbours is reduced, although the leader is, of course, responsible for ensuring that the pony remains amenable and reasonably still whilst the rider is attempting exercises. The occasional shifting of weight from one leg to another should not be scolded, providing the pony does not actually take a stroll across the arena at a crucial moment.

Should anything happen to cause alarm, such as a sudden squeal or the pony standing on your foot, do please try and count to ten before remonstrating with the pony. He probably did not feel your foot anyway and a sudden shout

or movement could mean the rider is unseated and un-
nerved, particularly if at the time he happens to be in the
middle of a difficult exercise.

A proven method of keeping the pony calm is to gently
rub your hand up and down under the crest of the mane,
with an occasional pat and a kind word. The voice is a great
soother and horses respond well to a calm reassuring tone,
regardless of what is actually said.

In spite of all your care and attention, it can still happen
that the disabled rider will lose balance and perhaps take a
fall at some time. Should this happen your first concern
must be for the rider. However, you should never let go of
the pony. If there is a side helper as well as a leader the
helper can assist the rider but if no helper is present the
leader should endeavour to help the rider regain balance
without letting go of the lead line. The instructor is always
on the lookout for such incidents and will quickly assist if
an emergency occurs. A loose pony in a ride can cause a
multitude of problems, whereas a single rider in trouble can
be coped with.

The leader can help the instructor and rider by continually
checking and reminding the student to keep the base of the
stirrup iron on the ball of the foot, so that if the rider does
fall the foot is not locked in the stirrup and we are spared
the nerveracking sight of a frightened pony and even more
frightened rider being dragged around the arena. Some
disabled riders, of course, find great difficulty keeping the
foot in a constant position whereas others use special stirrups, such as Devonshire boots or Peacock quick-release
stirrups, to help. If possible both feet should be removed
or knocked out of the stirrups if a fall looks likely.

When leading a pony and another rider falls or stops for
any reason, pull your pony up and stand perfectly still at a
good distance away. Turn and face your rider holding the
pony's head still by the reins on either side of the bit.

Never run to the aid of another rider unless instructed to
do so. It could result in a double fall and chaos. The

instructor or an assistant will help those who are in difficulties.

The leader is an indispensable part of every programme and is, in one respect, more important than the instructor, particularly for ensuring that all is well with horse and rider. Accidents have been known to happen and even an experienced pony can shy for no apparent reason, throwing the rider off balance.

It is not always possible, even for the fleetest-footed instructor, who is generally in the centre of the arena, to reach the pony in time. The leader can prevent such a thing happening, by anticipating and making sure the pony is held firmly and halted, with the rider assisted to regain his balance as quickly as possible. *Always expect the unexpected.*

The Side Helpers

It is the responsibility of the person at the side of the horse to help the rider maintain a sitting balance, prevent falls and encourage responsive activity.

Depending on the degree of ability, there may have to be a helper on either side. These helpers will have been briefed beforehand on each individual student's difficulty and requirements. Some riders will require to be held at all times, others at particular moments during the lesson and some hardly at all. The helper remains close at hand, however, as a safety precaution until the rider demonstrates the ability to ride independently without side assistance. At this time the leader at the horse's head assumes the role of leader and helper combined.

It is perhaps sad but true to say that leaders and helpers are working towards redundancy and should be proud of the day when they are no longer required for a particular student.

Helpers must always be alert and yet not over-anxious to assist the rider, who must be encouraged towards maximum self-help to be able to benefit from the exertion and following relaxation. If a loss of balance occurs, the rider should be assisted firmly and quickly without any sudden grabbing movement, that may frighten the student even more, particularly one with startle reflexes.

Riders who require to wear a body harness need more attention regarding posture control and balance recovery, hence the harness, but the temptation to hang onto the waist belt handles must be resisted. This habit, which seems to be catching with some helpers, can in fact cause unequal distribution of weight and subsequent loss of balance, which is not entirely the rider's fault.

Conversation between helpers and riders is, at times, beneficial to both, providing it does not interfere with the instructor's commands or distract the student. Excessive talking between helpers and leaders, or worse between another student's helper or leader, is a threat to safety and should not be allowed, except in an emergency. The instructor will direct leaders and helpers if he requires them to emphasise or repeat a certain point to the rider. They should not presume that he wants them to repeat everything he says to the student as a matter of course. Disabled riders must be credited with the intelligence they have and not presumed to be of lower intelligence simply because they happen to bear a physical disability.

Helpers and leaders must learn by experience to anticipate reactions from the horse and rider, to avoid accidents. It is particularly important to be observant and to watch for signs of fatigue on the part of the rider, which invariably causes a loss of concentration and coordination.

On the other hand, the helper must be persuasive and firmly but gently, without being over exuberant nor yet sentimental or condescending, encourage the rider to exertion and 'ride' the horse by himself.

Helpers and leaders should be, by virtue of their given knowledge and training, an extension of the instructor.

4 Mounting

The Ramp

It is very seldom that one finds a disabled student who is capable of mounting completely unaided in the accepted orthodox manner. Some means of assistance must be found to bring riders up from ground level to the horse's height without actually having to lift them bodily. Unless you are a confirmed weightlifter or an all-in wrestler, to attempt to lift up to six riders, one after the other, on to a pony or, even worse, a horse can be very strenuous and should not be attempted even by the fittest person, especially as it is very seldom that the student can help at all. (See notes on how to lift.)

For this reason it becomes necessary to build some type of ramp, especially for non-ambulatory riders who are dependent on wheelchairs or crutches. Various types are in current use but the most practical is the fixed, solid, double-sided wooden ramp that allows the horse to be led between the two sides, in one end and out the other (see diagram).

The ramp should have a gentle incline to the platform and be wide enough to allow a wheelchair to be pushed up and turned round on top without too much strain. If the rider uses crutches or a walking frame it should be possible to walk up the ramp with ease. At the top of the ramp, where the horse is halted, the platform should measure about 4 feet x 6 feet and its edges should be protected by tubular steel or wooden handrails on two sides.

Whether the rider is being mounted from a wheelchair or from crutches, the method of mounting does not alter a great deal. The chapter on leaders explained how to hold the pony, so it will suffice to say they must ensure that the horse is kept stationary while being mounted. The best

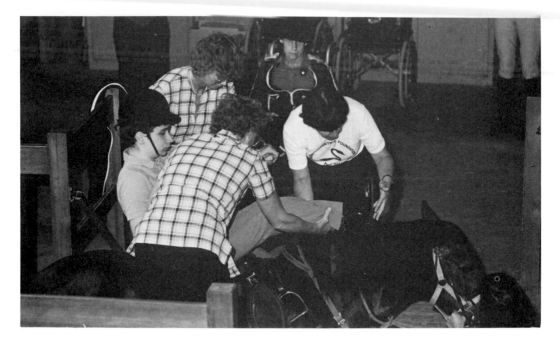

Fully assisted
mounting using a
ramp.

method is to stand directly in front, facing the horse, holding
a rein in each hand either side of the bit to avoid being
nipped, rather in the manner a racehorse is held, drawing
the rein out to either side and holding firm.

Should the leader stand to one side at this stage, then
there is a risk of the horse attempting to push past at an
inopportune time.

Before entering the ramp the horse's tack must be
checked, particularly the girth, to ensure that nothing is
loose or undone and that the saddle cannot slip round or over
the withers. It is the instructor's responsibility to personally
make a final check before the lesson commences. Special
pieces of equipment that may be in use should receive close
attention. D-straps or hand-holds, whether attached to the
D-rings at the front of the saddle or to the straps of the
girth, should be done up and adjusted as closely as possible
to the rider's natural hand position.

Numnahs or saddle pads, whether under or on top of the

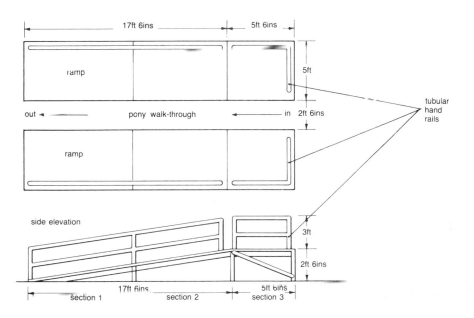

Mounting ramp. The ramp may be double- or single-sided, depending on space, etc. It can also be partitioned in three sections for ease in moving.

saddle, should be firmly fixed in place before the rider mounts. There are various ways of attaching saddle pads on top of the saddle for use by riders who are prone to suffer from pressure sores.

The adjustment of stirrups is very important for the safety and security of the rider and they should be correctly adjusted to the individual, bearing in mind that some disabled riders such as hemiplegics and amputees may require the stirrup length to be purposely odd.

If a body harness is used for younger riders with poor balance, it also should be correctly and comfortably fitted to the individual rider before mounting. The waistcoat or vest type of jacket with hand pockets on the back is the easiest to fit and adjust.

If a mobile ramp is being used it must be securely braked and blocked before the mounting procedure commences. Similarly an overhead hoist or bosun's chair-type lift should be secured out of harm's way before and after use.

New horses and ponies must be rehearsed frequently before putting them into regular work, with a groom acting as stand-in for the disabled rider, to get them used to being led in and out of the ramp and being mounted by rather unusual methods. To attempt to mount a green horse in the confined space on the ramp without first getting the animal thoroughly accustomed to it is courting disaster.

Great pains should be taken to ensure that there are not too many distractions, such as large groups of onlookers or objects lying about which could upset or frighten the horse. Wheelchairs and crutches, in particular, should be placed well out of the way as soon as possible to avoid them falling or knocking against the horse at a crucial moment.

The maximum number of people on the ramp at any one time should never be more than four: the leader on the ground, the rider, and if necessary two helpers, one on either side of the horse. Generally, one helper is sufficient except for riders with exceptionally poor balance. In most cases when mounting, this helper would be the instructor or assistant.

To prevent the pony from pulling backwards out of the ramp, a webbing strap can be hooked between the two sides, rather like the straps used on horse trailers. It should be fastened immediately once the horse has been led in. This precaution will avoid a nasty accident, which could happen if the pony happened to pull back as a rider was lifted.

Gradually, over a period of time, the horse can be moved further down the slope of the ramp until the rider can eventually mount, with or without assistance, from ground level.

Assisted Mounting

The method of assisting the rider to mount obviously varies according to the extent and type of the disability. Other considerations are the height, weight and age of the student,

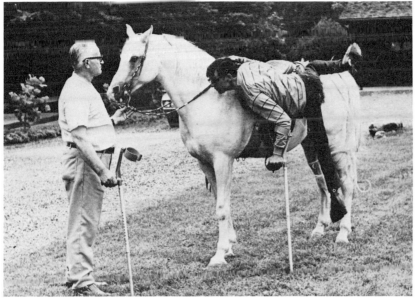

Unique way of mounting.

what help is available from volunteers and the size of the horse that is to be mounted.

Some riders who do not experience weakness or spasms in the lower limbs, can mount in the normal manner, given the height of the ramp. Some post-polio sufferers, lower-limb amputees and paraplegics have, in many instances, developed their upper body and arms to such a degree that they find vaulting onto the horse, even from the ground, a comparatively easy exercise. The unorthodox use of elbow crutches and walking sticks has also been used by a few individuals.

When using the ramp the horse must be held by the leader while being mounted, with the stirrups run up or crossed over the pony's neck in front of the saddle.

If students are capable of standing and walking, they should be assisted to the horse by the helper holding them under the left arm. Both hands should be placed on the pommel of the saddle, while the helper steadies the student by placing his hands on the rider's waist. The student then swings the right leg over, clear of the quarters, and lowers gently into the saddle.

Once seated comfortably, the neck strap or special hand hold attached to the D-rings should be held while both legs are lifted forward, by the helpers if necessary, until the horse is clear of the higher edge of the ramp. This method avoids the risk of the stirrup iron being caught under the platform.

Out of the ramp the stirrups can be adjusted to the individual and the feet placed in position before entering the riding area.

It must be emphasised that it may take some time for certain individuals to relax the leg sufficiently to the correct leg length required. Therefore they must be given time for the muscles to relax and the leg to lower. On no account must the leg be forced down into position because of impatience or lack of time.

It should be remembered that both sides of the horse should be tried for mounting, to determine the best method for the individual.

For riders with tight scissoring of the legs, spasms, or weakness, the method has to be changed a little. Many riders experience difficulty in bearing weight or being capable of stretching their knees or legs apart more than a few inches, and it would give them great pain at first to attempt to mount in the normally accepted manner.

From experience, it has been found that the safest methods of lifting a rider from a wheelchair are either by a total lift by one or two persons, or by a rider-assisted lift. The horse must be fully conversant with these unusual methods and frequently rehearsed.

Assisted Lift

At the top of the ramp the rider is lifted from the wheelchair by the instructor, who faces the student and puts his arms

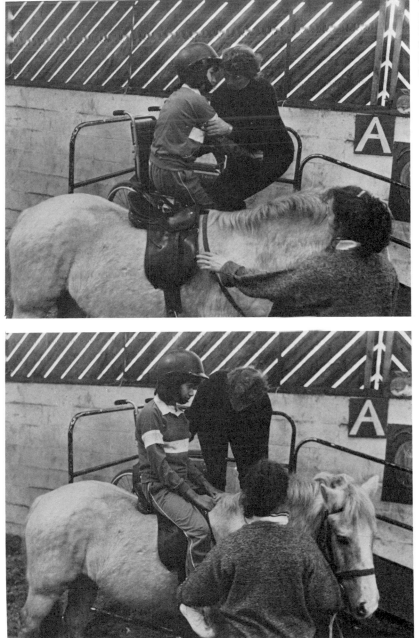

The pony waits
patiently side
helper at the ready,
while the rider is
helped into the
saddle.

under the armpits around the student's back. If the rider is capable he should also wrap both arms around the back of the lifter's neck. The instructor then places the right foot between both the rider's feet and bends his knees, keeping the back straight. To lift the student the instructor merely straightens and stands up. As he straightens, he must also turn so the rider's back is towards the horse. With the helper on the far side giving support, the rider is slowly lowered to the sitting position in the saddle.

Once seated, the legs are lifted in front of the student and the right leg slowly swung over to the off-side, with both legs bent forward of the saddle flaps until the horse is clear of the ramp. When clear, the rider's legs can be gradually drawn back to position and the knee slowly eased down into the knee roll and the feet slipped into the stirrups.

Total Lift from a Wheelchair

The chair must be positioned facing the horse on the near-side, level with the horse's hip, against the quarters. The brakes should be applied and the foot and arm rests pulled up or removed. If the student can self-assist by pushing down on one hand, then the arm rest on the far side can remain in place.

The lifter's arm is placed under the rider's knees, supporting the lower legs and buttocks while the right arm goes around the pupil's back under the armpits to hold the rider in an upright sitting position. The student can then be drawn forward from the chair onto the lifter's knees and from there to the hip. At this stage the wheelchair should be removed by a helper, behind the lifter.

The student can now easily be swivelled onto the horse by the lifter turning the hips towards the horse and straightening his knees. Depending on the individual and the disability, both the student's legs can be left either on the near-side or placed over the far side where they should be received and held by the helper until the rider is balanced.

Once the student is ready and relaxed, the legs can be divided and the feet positioned in the stirrups, ready to move off.

A heavier student may require two helpers to assist in the lift, while a third removes the wheelchair.

When mounting on the off-side and for dismounting, the system is reversed.

Assisted Mounting from the Ground

A few disabled riders may have sufficient physical ability to be capable of mounting from the ground. They should be encouraged to do so with maximum self-help and as little assistance as possible.

The quickest and safest method is the same as that used when helping an elderly lady or gentleman onto a hunter. Again a leader should be present at the horse's head, holding him steady.

Method 1. The rider should stand facing the horse's near-side, as close as possible, looking over the saddle. Holding the reins in the left hand, which rests on the pommel, the right hand should press down on the seat or centre of the saddle, or reach over, if possible, and grasp the far side at the skirt. The left leg is then raised and bent behind from the knee.

The helper should now take hold of the leg just below the knee with the left hand and above the ankle with the right. A count of three is given and on each count, the rider hops a little higher on the right foot. On the count of three, the lifter boosts the left leg up while the student swings his right leg clear of the horse's quarters and lowers gently into the saddle (taking care to move the right hand before sitting on it).

Method 2. Another method, favoured by riders who cannot bear weight on either legs, is the double leg lift. The student stands facing the horse in the same stance as method 1, with the hands also in the same position.

The helper bends at the knees with a straight back and grasps the rider firmly at both knees, locking them. With his shoulder under the student's buttocks, the lifter then straightens and turns towards the horse's head as he pushes the rider into the saddle, keeping both legs on the nearside.

A helper on the far side can steady the rider with a broad hand support until the student is balanced and the legs separated with the feet in the stirrups.

It should be emphasised that mounting is a very strenuous exercise and for this reason, unnecessary assistance should not be given to the student, nor any method used for the sake of speed or to make it easier for the rider.

When mounting a group of riders together who do not require assistance on the ground, the instructor should avoid mounting them in a bunch. Horses should be lined up at a good horse's length apart, particularly in an indoor arena or enclosed manège. All obstructions, such as jump wings, bending poles, and cavaletti must be placed out of harm's way.

Portable Mounting Ramps

When it becomes necessary for a group to take riders away from home for displays, competitions etc., a portable mounting ramp may be needed for those who would normally use the larger fixed ramp.

One type is the two-stepped, wooden and lightweight metal-framed platform on wheels, with hand rails on two sides, similar to the small steps used for boarding aircraft. This can easily be pushed by two people and once secured by the brakes or blocks is used for mounting in exactly the same way as with the larger ramp. There is not quite as much room on the top platform, so one helper only assists

A portable ramp.

while another, if necessary, stands on the ground or the far side of the horse.

Another type of portable ramp is made into sections, usually three, consisting of the top platform, the centre ramp and the lower ramp. Each piece is made of a lightweight wooden frame, with a marine-ply cladding, into which hand holds are cut on either side for easy carrying. All the sections can be locked into place once assembled, with rails dropped into slots on the far sides.

As with all ramps, the slope should have flat cross-battens or a ribbed, non-slip type of covering to prevent the person pushing the wheelchair (or the chair) from sliding backwards.

Hoists

Overhead hoists attached to wheeled pulleys in the roof or the mounting area, similar to a ship's bosun's chair, have been used by some groups with good effect for very over-weight students. Care must be taken, however, to ensure that they conform to a high standard of safety and efficiency and are regularly checked and maintained in good order.

When contemplating the use of this type of equipment, the instructor should consider the students' attitude and psychological reactions very carefully. Needless to say, the horse also requires special training to accustom him to this unusual method.

Basic Points when Lifting

(1) **Number of Lifters**. A light person may be lifted by one helper. If the student is heavy, two lifters should always be used. In exceptional circumstances three or more people may be required. The number of lifters should be adequate to avoid strain on either the lifters or the rider.

(2) **Choice of Lift**. Unless the student is completely help-less, the choice of the lift is in part decided by the nature of the disability and in part by the pupil's ability to assist in the movement.

(3) **Preparation for the Lift**. Having decided which lift to use, the lifters should arrange the area accordingly. There must be enough space beside the horse and nothing to trip the lifter. Get as close to the horse as possible. Where two lifters are used, ideally they should be of approximately the same height, the pupil midway between them. The lifter or lifters should then put themselves in the correct position so that the lift can be carried out smoothly, the pupil's arms having been arranged in a position suitable for the chosen lift.

(4) **Posture when Lifting**. Whichever lift is decided upon, the lifter should ensure that balance can be maintained

throughout the movement. If the correct posture is adopted, this will follow automatically. When lifting, the back should be straight, the chin tucked in and knees and hips bent, the thigh and hip muscles being used to straighten the legs and thus lift the patient.

(5) **Position of Feet**. This is very important in all lifting. The feet must be far enough apart to allow for balanced distribution of weight. If the pupil has to be carried, then as a general rule the lifter's leading foot should point in the direction of the move and the position of the other foot will vary according to the type of lift used and the stability required.

(6) **Grasps**. Grasps during lifting vary considerably but, in general, the broader the gripping surface the more secure the lift. Whenever possible, the whole of the hand should be used and the lifter's elbows should be kept close to the body.

(7) **Lifting Together**. To achieve a smooth and gentle lift, the lifters should lift at the same time on an agreed signal from one of them.

(8) **After Lifting**. As soon as the lift has been performed, the wheelchair should be moved away while the pupil is made comfortable. Any other articles such as crutches or sticks should also be moved out of the way of the horse before moving off.

(9) **Mounting Should Periodically Form Part of Every Lesson**. Pupils should not always be lifted, unless absolutely necessary. Find out the pupil's ability to help himself. Maximum possible self-help is essential for psychological, as well as physical benefit. Pupils should be encouraged to accomplish. Never hurry a pupil: take time and give time. Patience is essential. Always avoid embarrassment.

In the absence of a mounting block or ramp, there are various other ways of assisting the student who requires help in mounting, without actually having to bodily lift him. There may not always be volunteer helpers available, particularly if the rider dismounts (voluntarily or otherwise) when hacking out in the country.

Natural banks or ditches, wooden fences or stiles, tree stumps, or even mole hills provided they don't collapse, will give more height. Straw or hay bales, stacked logs, or animal-watering troughs, with care, can also be used to good effect with minimum assistance.

Unaided Mounting

It is possible in cases where the rider is not severely physically handicapped for him to be taught the correct method of mounting completely unaided.

The horse, however, should always be held by a helper while being mounted because the rider may not have sufficient strength to prevent the horse from moving at a crucial moment.

The method of mounting is the same as that recommended by responsible national horse organisations and taught by professional riding centres and schools throughout the western world. For handicapped students it is considered the quickest and safest method.

Before attempting to mount, the rider should be encouraged and taught to form the habit of checking all the horse's tack himself to ensure, for instance, that all strap ends are tucked neatly into keepers, buckles done up firmly, girth adjusted, and the stirrup leathers pushed firmly forward into the stays or bars on the saddle. The so-called 'safety clip' on most saddles should be left down, so that in the event of a fall, the leather will slide off.

Up until the time when the rider becomes independent,

Left: This purpose-built mounting block provides a sturdy platform from which to mount.

Below: Lightweight jumping blocks and a sturdy chair in use as mounting blocks.

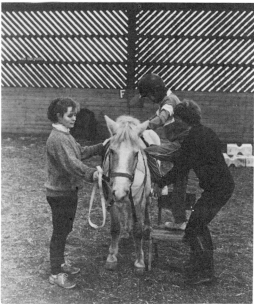

the instructor will have checked everything himself. It is recommended that periodically he continues to do so, or gets an assistant to do it, as the ultimate responsibility for safety remains his.

It must be emphasised to all instructors who teach disabled students that on no account should they skip or miss out little snippets of information or details of technique, which perhaps by themselves appear unimportant to the actual business of learning to ride. From experience, it will be found that pity is something the disabled rider does not want. Short cuts should be avoided and anything that would normally be included in a particular lesson should not be missed or glossed over.

Remarks such as, 'You need not concern yourself with this,' or, 'The helper will take care of that,' should be avoided. Little extra items of information can make a lesson so much more interesting and are, in most cases, welcomed by the rider who then feels more accepted.

Before mounting, the instructor should take the time to explain the different parts of the saddle and bridle, or the points of the horse for example, and he will find in most cases that he has an attentive class which, even with a group of perfectly healthy riders, can often be lacking.

The inability to accomplish a certain physical requirement, can be offset by the knowledge of how it should be done, and thereby lessen the degree of frustration.

The horse, having been led out with the stirrups run up and the girth initially adjusted, is held by the leader while the rider prepares to mount (see 'Stirrup Adjustment', p. 69, and 'The Girth', p. 70). Taking the stirrup iron in the right hand, the pupil eases it down the leather and draws it up under the left armpit, keeping the arm outstretched.

Placing the hand with the fingers bent at the second knuckle, he lays the hand on the bars under the skirt of the saddle and measures his approximate length of stirrup. The iron should rest under the armpit with the stirrup leather taut; if it is too loose or the iron does not reach under the arm then it should be adjusted. This method is only a rough guide to give an approximate length and the rider may have to readjust when mounted. Stirrups should be measured in this way, with the same arm either side of the horse.

To mount, the rider stands on the near-side facing the rear, with his left hip against the horse's shoulder. Reins are held in the left hand with the index finger between the two reins, making sure that the off-side rein is slightly shorter than the near, so as to prevent the horse from turning his head and nipping an unprotected posterior at a crucial moment. When a leader is holding the horse this painful incident is fortunately avoided, or should be!

With the left hand holding the reins resting across the horse's withers or on the pommel of the saddle, the rider takes the stirrup iron by the furthermost edge, turning it towards him. Raising the left leg he places the foot in the stirrup, making sure the toe is kept pushed down so that he does not dig it into the horse's side, which would annoy the animal and probably make him move forward. Once the left foot is in the stirrup iron the rider then hops around on the right foot, until he is looking over the far side of the horse and is able to reach over and hold the skirt of the saddle on the off-side, or if it is too far to reach he should hold the flap on the near-side where it joins the skirt.

The rider should never take hold of the cantle or back of the saddle, as this would cause it to slip forward making the underneath edge of the pommel press on the withers or if continually held in this manner could cause the tree or frame of the saddle to buckle or break. With practice he should soon be able to mount without holding or pulling with the right hand, but by pressing down on the seat of the saddle and straightening the arms as he jumps up, taking the weight of his body on his hands.

To get as close to the horse as possible before jumping up, the rider should keep the left knee pushed well out to the side towards the pony's shoulder.

The next stage is to hop on the right foot (the usual

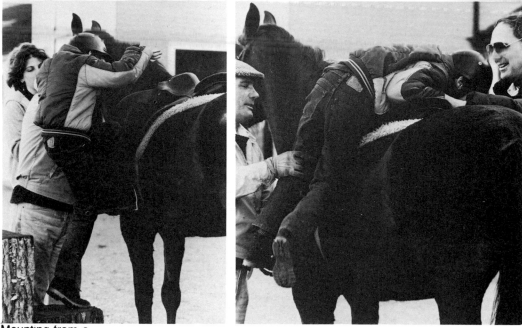

Mounting from a
block, assisted;
maximum self help
is encouraged.

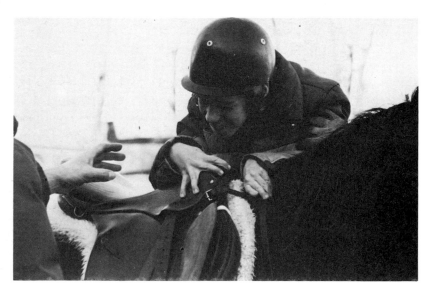

'There, you did it.'

The smile makes it
all worthwhile.

number is three times), gaining height each time and pressing down with the hands until taking the weight of the body on both hands, rather than on the left foot in the iron. Pivoting on the left stirrup iron and on his hands towards the pony's head, the rider swings the right leg straight out to the side and over, well clear of the quarters, making sure as he does so that the foot does not brush on the quarters which may once again startle the horse causing him to tip or buck.

As the seat is lowered gently into the saddle (and care must be taken to ensure that it is done gently), he moves the right hand away. The right foot is then slipped into the off-side stirrup, either by reaching down with the right hand and taking hold of the furthermost edge of the iron and turning it outwards or, with practice, knocking the nearest edge inwards and forwards with the toe and sliding the foot in as the iron turns.

If the stirrup iron is turned the wrong way and left so while riding, the edge of the twisted stirrup can cause a nasty sore on the inside of the calf, so make sure that the leather lies flat against the leg.

Dismounting

With disabled riders who cannot dismount without assistance, the horse should again be led into the fixed ramp, and the routine of mounting reversed. Make sure that both feet are taken out of the stirrups before entering the ramp, and that the stirrups are crossed in front of the saddle so the risk of their being caught on the edge of the ramp is avoided.

Riders of stronger physical ability, who are capable of dismounting correctly, should be taught the following way which has been proved to be the quickest and safest method.

The pony should be made to stand squarely, with his weight evenly distributed over all four legs; the rider then relaxes his feel or contact on the reins, and takes both reins bridged together in the left hand. Drawing both feet clear of the stirrups, he then bends forward from the waist, over his hands which rest on the pommel of the saddle.

With his weight on his hands as in a vault, the pupil throws the right leg back and up, keeping the knee straight, over the pony's quarters, swivels on the hands and drops lightly down on the near-side with the reins in the left hand, and stands facing over the pony's far side.

When dismounted the stirrups should be run up to the top of the leathers on both sides, and the loose ends tucked through the spaces on the bottom plates of the stirrup, to prevent the iron slipping down again. The girth should be slackened off to allow the horse to relax and the reins drawn over the horse's head, ready to lead off from the near-side.

Stirrup Adjustment

When mounted, riders should first of all check their stirrups to ensure that the length is correct for the particular form of riding they are going to do, that is, a longer length for school work, shorter for jumping. In cases where the rider is incapable or finds difficulty in adjusting his own stirrups and girth when mounted, the leader or helper must ensure that they are correct. Every effort should be made, however, to encourage the riders to do as much as they can by themselves.

Having made an approximate check before mounting, the stirrups should not need to be altered by more than one or two holes either way. To gauge the length required for ordinary school work the rider should remove the feet from the stirrups and let the stirrup leathers and his legs stretch down to their full extent. The bottom edge of the iron should knock just below the ankle bone if it is correct; if too far above or below then an alteration is needed.

Keeping both feet in the stirrups with the reins held in the free hand, the pupil takes hold of the leather just below the buckle and pulls up, drawing the buckle away from the bars in the recess on the saddle. The pressure of the foot in the iron should be relaxed slightly to allow the leather to run freely through the bars, then once the buckle is clear he is able to make any adjustment.

Pulling up the loose end, and at the same time pushing down on the stirrup iron with the foot, will release the point of the buckle from the hole. The rider can then alter the length by using hand and foot together to control the run of leather and by feeling and guiding the pin into the next hole required with the index finger.

Once an alteration has been made the buckle must be returned to its position against the bars in the recess, by taking hold of the underneath fold of leather with the hand and pushing down on the stirrup iron with the foot. The loose end should be tucked back towards the rear and held under the thigh muscle or tucked into the loop provided on the saddle flap.

The method of folding the loose end of the leather back under itself should be discouraged, as it forms quite a large lump under the knee, preventing grip or feel, and can cause a nasty sore on the inside of the knee if left there.

The Girth

Before mounting, the tension of the girth should be checked to ensure that the saddle will not slip round under the horse's belly at a crucial moment. Many a good rider having forgotten to do so has finished up sitting on the floor, and many a horse frightened by a saddle banging about in an unusual and unaccustomed position has bolted, with the rider dragged behind having a foot caught in the stirrup.

When the pony is first led out of the stable the girth will have been adjusted by the groom sufficient to keep the saddle central, but before the extra weight of a rider can be brought to bear on the stirrup irons the girth must be tightened. The leader or helper should ensure that this is done before a pupil attempts to mount, whether he mounts unaided or with assistance.

Before taking up the girth, the rider, if the leader is not present, must loop the left arm through the reins, making sure that the off-side rein is shorter than the near-side one, so as to prevent getting nipped by the horse as the girth is adjusted. Most horses resent the sudden tightening round their middle and very soon learn to show their disapproval, so the rider must be prepared.

The stirrup irons will have been run up to the top of the leathers against the bars or crossed over in front of the saddle out of the way.

To check the amount of adjustment needed the hand should be inserted between the girth and horse's side, forwards, inwards and downwards following the lie of the hair. If it is found difficult to force the hand behind the girth then it is too tight, or the pony has 'blown itself out'. An over-tight girth can cause soreness and eventually galls behind the elbow. If the horse is known to 'blow out' when being girthed up he should be walked around for a few minutes until he deflates and expels the air from his lungs before tightening.

The method often used of slapping the horse in the belly is never, in my experience, effective; in fact it only tends to make the animal fidget when the rider attempts to mount. If, when the hand is pushed behind the girth, it is loose and sloppy, then obviously it must be adjusted and the degree of tightness should only be sufficient to prevent the saddle moving when the rider mounts.

Once mounted and the horse 'warmed up' by walking and trotting for a few minutes, the saddle will settle down more into the pony's back and he will relax into regular rhythmic breathing, which allows the girth to slacken. It is at this stage that the final check and adjustments should be made.

The pony should be halted squarely and both reins taken in the right hand. The left leg is raised forward and up, keeping the knee as straight as possible with the toe pointing towards the pony's nose. Both feet should remain in the stirrups the whole time the alteration is being made.

Taking hold of the bottom edge of the saddle flap with the left hand, the rider lifts it up and draws it over the left thigh and holds it there with the right hand holding the reins. The girth straps are now exposed and by feeling with the left hand and guiding the pin into the next hole required on the straps, the girth can be taken up.

Once the adjustment has been made, pupils should make sure that the buckle guard is pulled back down over the buckles before dropping the flap back into place. Finally the leg is returned to its correct position and the reins taken up ready to walk on.

5 The Seat

'As we walk so will we ride,' is an old equestrian saying. It is very true that a person who normally slouches or humps the back is the same person that slumps in the saddle and looks down all the time when riding. With some disabled riders we have this problem twofold: not only do we have the crouching or slumped position, particularly with some cerebral palsy students, but it becomes far more difficult and takes much longer to correct. Very often when the body is corrected to an upright position, the legs will lift and we have in this particular disability the difficult task of trying to get the rider to use or correct one part of the body, or a limb, independently of the remainder. The instructor must therefore be careful to encourage what normal action there is and concentrate on building up the weaker muscles, while at the same time teaching the student to control those that over-react.

We are striving to teach all students to adopt the correct, balanced 'general-purpose' seat, but it must be recognised that it will be a very long, drawn-out process. We must be satisfied with even very slight improvements in posture, coordination and a sense of balance.

The training of the rider in the acquisition of balance is of the utmost importance and the instructor's principal task.

The movement of the horse brings about constant rhythmic motions, forwards, backwards, and sideways and, at times as in the trot, up and down. These changes in rhythm cause continual adaptions and corrections to be made by the rider to retain balance. From a steady, stable base at the halt the base changes to an unstable or insecure one, once the horse moves, or the rider is asked to perform an exercise. It is this constant correction of balance and recovery by the rider, trying to stay in unison with the horse that is probably the most therapeutically beneficial aspect of riding

In spite of the difficulties, we should endeavour to get the student to develop a reasonable position in the saddle, independent of the reins (or any other piece of equipment designed to hold on to) and concentrate on posture, balance and coordination of thought and deed.

The instructor's own judgment must be used, in consultation with the therapist, to determine how far and how quickly the rider can be expected to progress. It is noticeable that even very similar cases of a particular disability will vary greatly regarding their ability to adapt to the rigours of riding. No two individuals are alike and the instructor must determine the differences and the related problems during the assessment, and initial series of lessons. He must also ensure that the student fully understands what is expected, both mentally and physically.

Before getting the student to mount and sit in the saddle, the instructor should make certain that the right type of horse has been chosen if the rider is to be capable of eventually sitting correctly in the saddle, and obtaining a reasonably secure balance on a particular mount. Particularly with a cerebral palsy student, who may have tight scissoring of the legs, the width of the horse is of paramount importance. It is absolutely useless to expect a rider who finds it impossible to stretch the knees apart more than a few inches at first, to sit astride a wide-backed pony. The process must be gradual, starting with a narrow pony and changing to a wider girthed horse as the rider relaxes and becames better balanced and more proficient.

With post-polio cases, paraplegics, amputees and some others, the opposite is true, as they find the broader ponies an advantage in obtaining good posture, balance and subsequent easier application of the aids. The instructor does therefore have some flexibility in his choice of mounts and with experience can use various types and breeds as 'stepping stones' in the student's learning process.

It is obvious, of course, that all horses or ponies must be well schooled, up to the required standard, even-tempered and quiet in every respect. (See chapter on type of horse or pony.)

The method of teaching the 'balanced seat', (with the emphasis on balance) is as taught in all recognised professional riding establishments. The only difference here is that the rider, because of and depending on the extent of the disability, will take longer to acquire it. The instructor, therefore, would do well to ensure that the theoretical aspect of the lesson is first absorbed mentally, and then let the physical progression continue naturally, assisted by persuasion and continual repetition of exercises, which are designed to strengthen this particular and prime part of the anatomy and improve posture.

When we begin to teach the rider how to sit, we should simplify it by explaining and demonstrating, where, why, and how the rider should sit to develop the balanced seat. The word 'seat' means the student's position, and we should never expect or demand any two riders to be exactly the same or rigid copy-book examples. The students should be allowed to retain their individuality while we mould them into riders, not force them into stiff, moronic, unbending, dumb jockeys.

In the first few lessons we are aiming to teach feel, balance, and suppleness, combined with the ability to learn how to influence the horse in rhythm with the movement, by the action of the body and the application of the aids. The rider must, therefore, be taught to sit as close as possible to the horse's back, in the centre of the saddle, to be capable of feeling and controlling the forward impulsion from behind.

The saddle, regardless of the type or size, forms a barrier between the rider and horse and for a novice it is difficult to be able to make contact or 'feel' through the legs and seat, particularly when concentrating on merely staying on.

Bareback riding, on the lunge, with a vaulting surcingle, or with just a blanket covering, is the fastest way to learn balance and feel, but it can be tiring and is a very strenuous form of exercise to any but the fittest and more courageous of riders, and should not be attempted too soon or for too lengthy periods.

For some disabled pupils, particularly cerebral palsy, spastic types who experience difficulty in stretching the legs apart and have uncontrollable muscle spasm, it has been found that allowing them to ride in this fashion or on a thin saddle pad, is of tremendous benefit. The warmth of the horse through the pad, combined with the rhythmic movement, acts like a constant massage that relaxes the muscles and allows the legs to extend so that feel and balance improve.

An English saddle with a deep central seat is ideal for teaching correct posture. Some flat-backed saddles and the Western type tend to throw the rider's weight too far back, making a straight spine and correct leg position difficult.

In the beginning the rider should be taught to feel with the seat bones for the deepest part of the saddle between the cantle and the pommel. By taking hold of the front of the saddle with both hands and stretching down either side of the horse with both feet out of the stirrups, the rider can work the seat down and forward into the saddle. The knee and inside thigh muscles should be pushed downwards and inwards into the knee roll, close to the saddle flap.

If the rider is unfortunate enough to carry an over-generous amount of thigh muscle, which could hinder the close contact that is required, then this method should divert it away to the back of the thigh; if not, then the pupil must draw it away behind with the hand. A vice-like grip in any part of the leg should be avoided, as over-tension of the leg muscles will lead to stiffness, cramps or spasms that will affect the rider's ability to transmit the aids.

To be in complete unison with the movement and balance of the horse the rider must attempt to adopt a position that corresponds with the centre or line of gravity of the horse, which runs vertically through the horse's back and chest, halfway between the fore and hind legs. He should avoid collapsing or rounding the back, allowing the weight to rest on the base of the spine, which could cause him to be left behind the forward movement. Similarly he should avoid any stiffening of the muscles or a hollow in the back which could throw the weight too far forward onto the crotch.

A triangle, the base of which runs across the knees and from the knees to a point at the base of the spine, is the area in the centre of which the rider's weight should rest, directly over the seat bones, which is the horseman's name for the pubis or pelvic bone. Once the seat is firmly down in position, and it will take many hours of practice for it to sink naturally when mounted, the pupil must then endeavour to correspond the remainder of his body to the vertical line.

Moving up from the feet resting on the stirrup iron, which should lie across the ball of the foot just behind the toes, the rider should be encouraged to keep the heels below the level of the toes with the weight on the instep or inside edge of the iron and the foot turned slightly out away from the horse, more or less the natural angle when walking. If the foot is turned outwards too far, the calf muscle at the back of the leg will be forced to grip the horse's side unnecessarily, perhaps causing him to fidget in the first instance and to eventually become unresponsive to the finer leg aids.

From the knee downwards the lower leg should be drawn back into the natural line as when standing, lying just behind the girth close to the horse's side without gripping. Above the knee to the hips the thighs stay close to the saddle as already described and daylight should not be seen between the knees and knee rolls or flaps.

The rider must endeavour to remain upright, as if sitting in a straight-backed chair. He should not, however, show any stiffness but relax his muscles yet without collapsing either forwards or backwards which would put extra strain

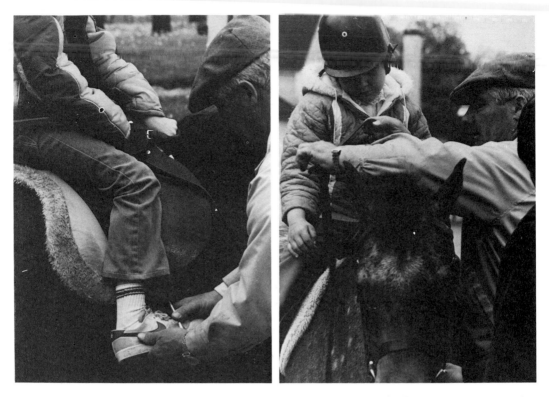

Above left: Having adjusted the stirrup length the foot is correctly positioned in the stirrup iron.

Above right: Explaining how to hold the reins.

onto the spine. With the shoulders facing squarely to the front, the head should be held erect, feeling the collar on the back of the neck, while the rider's gaze should be focused forwards approximately one length ahead of the horse. Should he look down at his hands or the horse's ears, which seem to hold a peculiar fascination for some pupils, this will force the back muscles to stiffen, creating a forward, false position.

The arms should hang naturally down the sides with the elbows resting against the waist just above the hip bone. From the elbow the arm is bent following a line running down the arm through the wrist and reins towards the horse's mouth.

The rider must be taught to avoid bending or 'breaking' the wrist which would tend to force the hands outwards.

He should be encouraged to maintain a slight inward curve of the fingers and wrist, without tucking them in towards the stomach – a method often adopted by novices which can cause loss of contact through the reins.

The hands hold the reins by letting the leather run up between the little finger, inside the middle three and over the top of the index finger, held or locked by the thumb, with the loose end dropped forward and inside the taut rein running to the bit, on the near-side. With the hands kept just above and in front of the pommel of the saddle, approximately 4–5 inches apart (the width of the horse's mouth), and the thumbs pointing to opposite ears, the rider endeavours to feel the pony's mouth as if holding a length of elastic, maintaining an even flexible contact with supple wrist and fingers. On no account must they be allowed to use the reins for support or to maintain balance, a neck strap or the special D-strap attached to the D-rings on the front of the saddle is used in the early stages for this purpose.

Correct method of holding the rein, and correct curve of wrist, viewed from above.

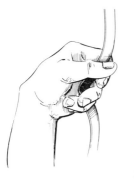

Overbent wrist (*far left*) and 'broken' wrist.

It is obvious that many disabled riders will find difficulty at first, and some may never really obtain the ideal position in the saddle, or be capable of applying the 'correct' aids. It is noticeable that spastic cerebral palsy students, for example, may not be capable of bending adequately at the hips to sit in an upright position. To compensate for this they may round their backs. To help this type of student, the stirrups can be shortened to give more pressure on the foot which will aid the joints to bend more easily.

Some other cerebral palsy students may suffer with a sway back and the instructor must encourage a slightly rounded lower back position to avoid increasing the sway.

Similarly when teaching the spastic student to hold the reins, an alternative method must be used, rather than the normally accepted practice of flexing the wrists and holding the reins between flexed fingers. The pattern of flexion should, wherever possible, be broken and extension encouraged.

Students who suffer with a curvature of the spine (scoliosis), post-polio, spina bifida etc., may tend to sit or lean to one side, so it is important that the instructor continually checks to ensure that a deep central position is held. The best position to observe whether the rider is sitting centrally with the weight evenly distributed on both sides, is by standing behind the horse as he moves away.

Hemiplegics, as already stated, may need stirrups to be purposely odd, to encourage use of the weak side. Similarly, riders who flex the knees or who may have had surgery and find difficulty in bending joints, may be allowed to ride with longer stirrups.

Those who must continue to wear callipers or braces when riding, will also require a longer stirrup. Consultation with the therapist will determine the necessity of removing or retaining these when mounted. Other abnormalities such as flexed joints, tight heel cords, and feet turned in or out, will affect the rider's ability to obtain the required position.

The instructor should frequently consult with the therapist and use good judgment in determining how complete a position he can demand or expect. The ultimate he strives for is to give the rider the ability to control the horse by his own efforts, irrespective of perfection in posture or balance, so long as the end result does not irritate or harm the horse and is not a threat to safety.

6 Special Equipment

Because of the numerous difficulties that have arisen with the handicapped using standard riding equipment, it has become necessary over the years to adapt, invent and develop special items of equipment that make riding possible for certain individuals who otherwise would not be able to participate.

Special gadgets should not be thrust upon disabled riders to make it easier for them or their helpers or quicker for the instructor. If it is possible for students to ride with normal equipment, even though it may be with some difficulty, they should be encouraged to use it.

The fact that it may be difficult is all the more reason for the student to make the extra effort. If something is impossible, or highly unlikely, at first for the rider to accomplish, then some special piece of equipment may have to be used initially. If, for example, it is impossible for a student to mount normally, but with the stirrups let down to the full extent of the leather he can mount from the ground, even with difficulty, he should be encouraged to try. The ramp or total body lift should not be used to make it easier or faster.

In the process of learning and improving one should always be working towards normality, so constant re-evaluation by the therapist and instructor should take place.

Certain items will, nonetheless, stay with the student for some considerable time regardless of the disability. Lead lines, hand holds and, in some instances, saddle pads or protectors, are examples.

The instructor should first consider the reasons for normal equipment and riding wear, which are designed for comfort and to protect the rider from injury. Correctly tailored clothing also assists the rider in influencing and controlling the horse.

If it is possible for the student to wear the correct attire, they should be encouraged to do so, as they would for any other sport. On the other hand, if the disability or some necessary item of equipment, such as callipers or braces, prevent a correct fitting, they can be more casual.

Loose-fitting clothes, particularly covering the legs, can cause rubbing and eventually sores that can be bothersome. Therefore if casual clothing is worn, advice should be given on its fitting to prevent these little aggravations. This also applies to boots, shoes and hats.

Boots and shoes should be of strong leather, with support to the ankle and some protection to the front of the foot where the stirrup may rub. Low heels and rubber soles are advisable. Long boots can be worn by many if a zipper replaces the back seam to make them easier to remove and pull on.

Hats are the main safety item and should, of course, fit correctly and be comfortable, with sufficient padding inside to ensure they stay in place. Those fitted with a harness, and preferably without a peak, are safest. Because they probably receive the roughest treatment, hats should be inspected at regular intervals for signs of wear or weakness and replaced if necessary.

It has been noted by most national authorities that no particular make or design of hat has been found ideal. It is recommended that care should be taken when fitting a hat to a hydrocephalic or spina bifida student, who may already have to wear some form of protective headgear.

The following guidelines apply to the use of special riding equipment:

(1) Only use when absolutely necessary.

(2) Do not use beyond the student's need.

(3) Never attach to horse and rider at the same time.
(4) It should not interfere with the rider's balance, movement or control.
(5) It should not cause any embarrassment.
(6) It should not restrict or cause any discomfort or injury to the horse.

In the choice of equipment other considerations that should be discussed at the initial assessment and thereafter periodically include:

(1) The type and extent of the disability and whether it is stable, progressive, or improving.
(2) The age, health and physique of the student and the physical and mental expectations.
(3) The student's knowledge, experience and attitude toward riding.
(4) The student's temperament, character and ambition.
(5) The frequency, length and form of lessons.
(6) The breed, size and number of mounts to be ridden.
(7) The extra cost and the amount of finance available.

The items that are listed in the remainder of this chapter constitute those that have been found useful over the years for a variety of disabilities. No individual item is prescribed specifically for a certain individual and it is up to the instructor, in consultation with the therapist, to determine the individual's need at the initial assessment.

The Body Harness or Safety Belt

Probably the most widely used item of special equipment, particularly for small children and beginners with poor balance or weak posture, is the adjustable body harness or safety belt.

It was developed at Chigwell to be worn in the early stages of riding so that an assistant can help the pupil maintain

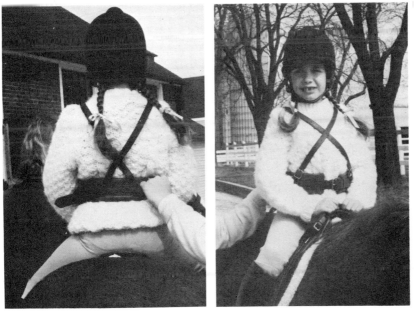

Body harness, front and back views.

posture and recover from a loss of balance in any direction. The side helper assists by holding onto handles on the belt or by grasping the cross-over shoulder straps. This does away with the uncomfortable and embarrassing need to grab handfuls of the rider's clothing.

The belt part of the harness can be made of soft lampwick material or folded soft leather, roughly 3–4 inches wide and 22 inches long for children, with adjustable leather straps and buckles in front. Attached to the wide belt are two adjustable cross-over shoulder straps, similar to a baby's carriage harness, and two leather handles on either side at the back.

Helpers must be taught not to hang onto the handles continually as this would tend to pull the rider off balance or make them over-dependent on the support.

As the pupil improves, the use of the belt, and indeed any special equipment, can be gradually discontinued until it can be eventually dispensed with altogether, once the rider is capable of maintaining a good balanced position alone. Small children in particular find the body harness very reassuring and do not resent wearing it

A waistcoat or vest-type jacket has been developed in the United States recently, with broad upside-down pockets in the back into which the helper puts the hand to give support.

It is worth noting that the broader the area covered by the harness or jacket, the greater the support. A waist belt alone does not prevent the upper torso from tipping off balance quite so effectively.

Students with minimal use of their lower limbs and those with either very flaccid or spastic muscles will benefit from this support.

Saddle Pads (Numnahs)

Pupils with spinal damage and weakness, or those who suffer from defective sensations in their legs and seat area and have little natural padding, will require something to protect them against saddle or pressure sores. Sheepskin or even synthetic numnahs or saddle pads are expensive and difficult to clean, particularly if the student is incontinent. There is also a tendency for them to slip on top of the saddle even when tied securely, so perhaps they are better left underneath the saddle where they were meant to be.

An inexpensive pad that is soft, washable, and can be fitted easily and securely to the saddle, can be made quite quickly by any average seamstress. The first two used at Chigwell were made by the mother of a handicapped student in one afternoon.

A soft canvas bag the same shape as the saddle pad, is made with a zippered opening in the front seam about 12 inches long with two 1 inch slits in the side flaps where the stirrup bars are. On the underneath side, two half flap pockets are made. At the back of the bag on the under side, a rounded 2–inch gusset is sewn, which can be pulled over the cantle, or back, of the saddle to prevent the bag from slipping forwards. The bag is filled with 1-inch thick Sorbo sponge cut to the same, but slightly smaller, pattern.

The whole pad is held in place by the saddle flaps pushed into the bag pockets and the stirrup leathers tucked through the slits before attaching them to the saddle. The weight of the rider and pressure on the stirrup irons prevents the bag from moving. This type of pad does not require the use of a surcingle or messy tapes to keep it secure, yet it does give the rider adequate comfort and protection from pressure sores without interfering with the necessary close contact.

For riders who may require a little more back support, it is quite a simple matter to fill out the back of the pad with an extra roll of sponge.

Felt or cloth-filled pony pads can be used in place of a saddle by children with spastic muscles and tight scissoring of the legs. The warmth and massaging effect of the pony is of great benefit in decreasing the muscle tension and lengthening the legs. Pads with fixed stirrups and girth attachments are preferred, with an overgirth used for safety, as they do tend to slip sideways.

Recently the Dycem plastic non-slip mat, which is the size of an average dinner plate, has been used to good effect in preventing riders from slipping on a shiny saddle. The pad sticks firmly in place and grips the rider's seat. It also gives added protection to the saddle and is softer for the rider. Therapists can obtain them from clinic, hospital or therapy department suppliers, as they are used for a multitude of purposes.

Stirrups

It has been found an advantage with certain students to use curved or off-set stirrups, or those with a tilted base plate to encourage downward heel flexion.

Peacock safety stirrup with snap-off rubber band attachment, and (*far right*) Devonshire boot.

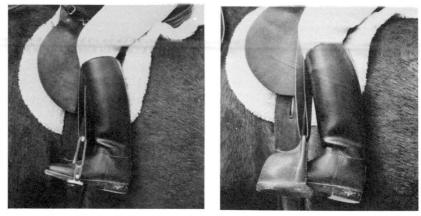

Peacock safety stirrups, with the snap-off rubber-band attachment, are particularly useful to riders with weakness in the lower limbs, specifically for post-polio, spina bifida, paraplegics, and lower limb amputees. They are also ideal for students who suffer from a lack of sensation or who may not be aware of the position of the foot.

Some establishments recommend the Peacock stirrups for all disabled students. However, there is a tendency for the rubber bands to come loose and the foot to slide out if too much pressure is put on the outside edge, particularly at the trot. The type that combine a leather loop and a smaller rubber ring will last longer and are more efficient. The risk of the rider being dragged by the stirrup in the event of a fall is avoided by this safety measure.

The Devonshire boot is also available as standard equipment and not really considered peculiar to the disabled. Similarly the Devonshire boot encourages downward heel flexion and enables the iron to be kept on the ball of the foot when it is thrust right home. The stiff leather 'boot' that projects out from the stirrup iron, also affords protection to the toes from cold and knocks as well as preventing the foot from slipping through the open stirrup.

With increasing costs of equipment, the same effect can

be obtained by bolting a bicycle pedal spring toe-clip onto the bottom plate of the stirrup.

Standard rubber stirrup grips in the base of the iron give greater adhesion and help the rider maintain a correct and safe foot position, so long as the foot is not pushed all the way home. Students affected by tight heel cords or contractions should not use the rubber grips but would do better with the Peacock stirrups or Devonshire boots.

If difficulty is experienced in keeping the feet in the stirrups, particularly with mis-shapen or larger than normal boots, it may be advisable to dispense with stirrups alto-gether. This also applies to lower limb amputees provided the false limb is well secured.

It is extremely dangerous and not recommended for riders to ever be allowed to put their feet into the fold of leather above the stirrup.

For ease of mounting, the special let-down stirrups are readily available from good saddlers and prevent the nuis-ance of having to make time-consuming adjustments with the buckles.

Reins

Some students by nature of their disability have great diffi-culty in grasping the reins in the correct manner, so to enable them to control the 'forehand' a number of special types of reins have been developed.

The looped rein has three rounded leather loops or handles stitched onto either side of the reins approximately 6 inches apart. The loops are large enough to slip the whole hand in and out easily (rather like the loops on a ski stick), using the wrist or back of the hand to steer. The length of rein required determines which loop is used.

The ladder rein, as its name implies, has three or four

Looped reins.

'rungs' of rolled leather at intervals of 6 inches apart, starting approximately 1 foot down from the buckle end and joined on either side. To shorten or lengthen the reins, the rider simply moves up or down a rung. They were developed at Chigwell specifically for riders with deformed or weak hands, or for riders with false limbs or hooks, who were incapable of holding standard reins. Riders with a weak grasp or uncontrolled limb movements also find the reins helpful.

Other advantages are that they prevent the horse from suddenly lowering its head to graze when working on a grassy area, and the rungs are always in reach because of the way they straddle the horse's neck.

It is not advisable to jump a horse using these reins because they can be restrictive to the lowering and extending of the neck, if the rider is slow to give. At least one member of the English aristocracy, however, who is also disabled, regularly hunts with them and is featured in an excellent film available from the British Riding for the Disabled Association entitled 'The Right to Choose'.

There are various kinds of non-slip reins, either rubber covered or webbing with leather stops, that are preferred by some students to the ordinary straight leather ones, providing they are not too bulky or thick. The **'Humes' rein**, developed in the United States at the Wayne Du Page Hunt programme for exceptional children, has only two loops at the buckle end and is adjustable at both sides for the individual horse and rider.

Ladder reins. To shorten the rider simply moves down a rung.

It may sometimes be necessary to have normal reins deliberately cut shorter by a foot or more, according to the size of the mount. This makes them easier to manage and avoids the possibility of feet or stirrups becoming entangled in the long loose end. The practice of knotting the end of long reins is not really satisfactory, as the knot itself can become caught under the hand hold or between the student's knee and the saddle.

With thalidomide and some other disabilities, the suggestion of tying or fixing the reins to shorter limbs, or placing them around the rider's neck or body is highly dangerous and should not be contemplated. If difficulty is experienced with steering by the hands, it may take a little longer to teach, but it would be better and much safer to instruct these students in the art of guiding the horse from the stirrups using their feet and body weight in the same way as the mounted musicians and drummers of the Household Cavalry do.

Grass or overhead check reins can be simply made up from lengths of twine or even hay string tied to the saddle D's, run up the horse's neck, through smaller metal D's at the corners of the browband and attached to the rings of the snaffle. These 'check reins' prevent the horse from snatching at grass and pulling the reins out of the student's hands, or, worse, pulling the rider out of the saddle and off balance. Professionally made nylon check reins have a spring clip at the bit end and are adjustable.

The method of passing the cord through the leather loop at the corners of the browband, prevents the necessary free-running action of the rein. The fitting of the D's thereby alleviates the likelihood of the reins becoming caught up and causing injury to the pony's mouth through sudden jerking.

Side reins, with elastic or rubber rings let into the leather to give greater flexibility, can be used in place of check reins, particularly for larger ponies or horses that are ridden by heavier adolescents or adults, initially on the lunge.

Side reins again deter the animal from suddenly pulling the rider off balance through the reins. They also help to keep the bit central in the horse's mouth and thereby prevent a rider, who may be stronger in one hand, from pulling the bit through to one side. Round rubber bit stops are also ideal for avoiding this common occurance, as well as reducing the risk of sores at the corners of the horse's mouth.

Side reins and overhead check reins must be correctly fitted and the horse worked in them to ensure acceptance before the rider is mounted. Similarly, in the interests of safety, they *must* be detached before dismounting.

Hand Holds

In the early stages of learning to ride, when balance and posture are so important, it is essential that anyone who cannot control the reflex action of the hands or has poor balance, should have something other than the reins or saddle to hold on to or to reach for in an emergency. The reins should not be given to a rider who is likely to hurt the horse's mouth, through no fault of his own. For beginners and those who have difficulty with precise arm and hand control, it is recommended that the reins be attached to a headcollar worn under the bridle. This will avoid unnecessary harm to the horse's mouth.

Equally, if a student is allowed to hold onto the pommel of the saddle, the fingernails can cause the horse some discomfort and irritation in that very sensitive area in front of the withers, particularly if fingers are repeatedly being dug into the hair and pulling on it. The crest of the mane at this point is very sensitive and continual aggravation can cause a violent shaking reaction that can unseat the rider.

There are people who advocate using the mane as a hand hold but again, continual usage can cause soreness and eventually bald patches which are most unsightly. However, in an emergency or when teaching the rising trot or the forward jumping position, it can be used briefly to good effect.

Whatever the type of handle, it must be remembered that not only should it be strong and secure enough for the rider to rely on, but it should be positioned in such a way that it assists the rider to maintain the required natural position of the hands and body.

D-straps, approximately 12 inches long, made of rolled leather, with either spring clips or adjustable buckles at the end, can be attached to the metal D's on the front of the saddle. Alternatively, for heavier riders, a 26–inch handle made the same way, but with leather loops at the end, can be slipped over the front girth or billet straps.

The use of an old stirrup leather as a neck strap is not very good by itself, as the strap tends to slip around the horse's neck, particularly if the rider is a little one-sided.

A D-strap fitted to the front of a saddle provides a useful hand hold.

This can be avoided by stitching an additional rolled leather handle onto the top of the strap and then attaching the whole thing to the saddle D's with twine or nylon cord tied either side of the handle. This will prevent the strap from moving but is it inclined to be cumbersome and a little untidy.

Rigid metal or wooden handles have been used that are welded or screwed to the front pommel of the saddle. These are dangerous and can injure the rider, particularly at the faster paces or when the rider has to bend forwards in exercises. This type of handle is not therefore considered suitable, or indeed, necessary for any disabled student.

Leading Reins

In the beginning nearly all disabled students will have to be led until they are capable of riding alone.

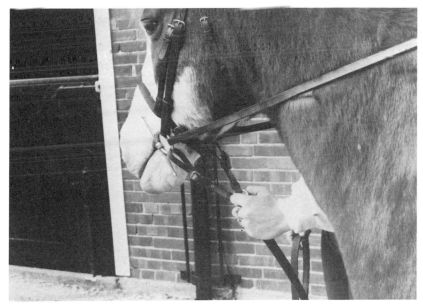

A double lead line
fitted directly on to
the bit.

There are two main types of lead line in current use:

The double lead line helps to avoid the possibility of the pony's mouth being damaged by a beginner's hands and yet, at the same time, gives the rider a certain amount of contact or feel through the reins.

The leather line divides from a ring at one end into two adjustable straps which are then attached to each ring of the snaffle bit below the rider's reins. The leader holds the rein at the ring where it divides, with the hand nearest the horse, while the other end of the line is looped and held by the leader in the hand farthest from the pony. This gives the leader much more control over the pony and also prevents the rider from jerking too hard on the bit. At the same time the student can feel through his own reins and soon learns to follow the movement of the pony's head with his hands, without losing the contact.

Because it is attached to the bit, the double lead line is,

Leading rein
attached to the
back of the
noseband.

of course, a good deal more severe, it is essential that the
leader should exercise care when using it.

The single leading rein is made either of leather or webbing
with a looped hand hold and a buckle and strap at the
pony end that can be fastened to the back of the cavesson
noseband. The practice of fixing the buckle to one ring of
the snaffle is not recommended as it creates too much of a
nutcracker action with a jointed snaffle and increases the
pressure on the bars of the horse's mouth with a straight
bit.

Saddles

A well-made modern, deep-seated general-purpose saddle is
the ultimate for a disabled student as it is for any beginner
rider. Not only is it essential for giving the student a sense
of security from the outset, but it also assists in the all
important problem of maintaining balance and posture. The
more firmly entrenched the pupil can become and the closer
he can get to the horse, the sooner he will learn to feel and

to follow the forward movement and eventually become a competent rider, which is, of course, the ultimate aim.

It is ridiculous to expect anyone to be capable of maintaining a good posture or balance on a flat-backed or forward-tipped saddle, that either throws the body too far forward over the forehand or backwards over the loins, when the horse moves off.

Elsewhere it has been mentioned that certain disabled students benefit greatly from the warmth and rhythm of the horse through riding bareback with a felt pad or blanket. Other riders such as paraplegics or post-polio sufferers may require additional support from rolled padding over the cantle which fits into the small of the back. Western or military types of saddles do give greater support both in front and behind but they are restrictive for exercises and they do tend to put an unnatural strain on the base of the spine, because of the length of stirrups required.

Whatever the type of saddle or support that is used, however, it should not completely take over from the rider's own ability to support himself. Students must endeavour and be encouraged to maintain balance and posture by their own natural means.

The safety of the student must always be uppermost and on no account should anyone be strapped in by any method other than the type of fitting that will separate when extraordinary pressure is applied.

Basket saddles for children are not recommended when teaching the basics of riding, because they completely take away the need for the pupil to use his own muscles to maintain balance and give a false impression of the horse's movements. Furthermore the child is more often than not firmly strapped in and is, therefore, incapable of freeing himself in time to avoid serious injury if the pony falls. The sides and back of the saddle are also restrictive for anything but the simplest of exercises.

Regardless of the type or actual design of the saddle, the

physiotherapist's advice should be sought in cases of doubt regarding an individual disability.

Miscellaneous Equipment

Riding crops or sticks obviously should not be given to handicapped riders who cannot control their own limbs or who have not reached the stage of learning where they can appreciate the need and use of these items. Students with artificial limbs or weakness in the legs can, however, be taught the correct use of the schooling whip to reinforce the aids once they have reached the required stage of advancement.

On the subject of aids, it is worth repeating that the instructor should not be too dogmatic concerning any fixed ideas on teaching diagonal or lateral aids. The application of either one or the other for any particular individual can mean the difference between the student becoming proficient or frustrated with his own accomplishments. Adaptability is the keynote!

Knee bandages or athletes' elastic knee trusses are particularly useful for riders with weak joints or lack of control over their legs. Covering the knees helps close contact when it is required to prevent a loss of balance and at the same time it assists the pupil in keeping the leg in a firm position for applying the aids. Bandages over the knees also prevent rubbing and soreness that can be caused by the unaccustomed movements.

A bell, similar to those fixed on a kitten's collar, can be attached to the back of the saddle of the leading horse for blind students to follow the sound. This is of particular benefit when orientating students to the indoor arena and indispensable when hacking out.

Other items of equipment such as mounting blocks or ramps, pulleys and surcingles are dealt with elsewhere.

In conclusion it must be remembered that students must enjoy the experience of riding and if they are encumbered with too many gadgets or pieces of equipment this may cause some concern and detract from the aim. None of the special pieces of tack is designed to completely replace standard equipment. As soon as it is possible for the student to change to normal equipment they should be encouraged to do so. The basic principles of instruction and equitation should always be uppermost in the mind of the instructor and should be interfered with or changed as little as possible.

7 The Exercises

In all recognised riding establishments that give qualified instruction, exercises on horseback form a basic and very important part in the elementary stages of learning to ride. They give the rider confidence, a sense of balance and coordination, and teach him how to use his body and muscles naturally, with the minimum amount of force or tension in asking the horse to obey his signals or aids.

Once the pupil is past the elementary stage and has achieved a certain degree of suppleness and know how, so that he is capable of transmitting his intentions to the horse smoothly, the exercises in an average riding school are all too often forgotten. The instructor then concentrates on teaching the rider not only to improve his own riding ability, by correcting obvious faults in position etc., but also how to educate or school the horse to a higher degree of obedience by putting the animal through more complicated and vigorous movements by a finer and more subtle application of the aids.

It is very rare that exercises are continued as part of a lesson, except voluntarily by the rider, once he is capable of maintaining a secure balanced seat at all paces and is able to negotiate a varying course of jumps or execute elementary dressage movements in an enclosed arena.

With disabled pupils, the riding instructor must realise that it is practically impossible to expect them (except in rare cases) to ever be sufficiently in control of either their own body or the horse to be able to educate or school the horse any further. In fact it has been found that horses and ponies frequently need re-schooling by the instructor, after a long period of being ridden by disabled, as the horses tend to become bored and to disregard the aids.

Disabled riders also have the usual bad habit, as have all riders who take it up for the first time, of using the reins as a means of support in trouble, with the resulting hard mouth to contend with, plus the annoying bit evasions common with mishandled or badly bitted ponies.

Unlike riders who have no physical disability, and who soon become proficient at performing exercises, the disabled rider continues to be 'put through it' even after he has been riding for some considerable time. In fact the exercises are very often done on practically every lesson for as long as he continues to attend classes.

The reason for this is simply that the instructor, in teaching the pupil to ride, is not only concerned with his riding ability, although of course his ultimate aim is to make him as proficient a rider as he can, but also he must concentrate on developing that particular part of the rider that is affected, making him use it so that it gradually becomes useful and strong once again. With spastic pupils, however, it is not so much a question of making the muscles stronger but giving the rider the ability to control them.

The instructor should never advertise the fact to other pupils, or anyone else not closely concerned, that he knows the extent of the pupil's disability, but should make all his pupils attempt all the exercises without forcing them irrespective of whether or not they are in actual fact capable of doing them particularly well, provided of course the exercise does not do them any harm. Consultation with the resident medical consultant or physiotherapist will determine this.

Because a rider cannot at first straighten an arm it does not necessarily mean he will not eventually be able to do so, with persistent coaxing and perseverance. Never be witty, sarcastic or hold up to public view the rider's disability. It will not benefit you or your pupil, in fact it will certainly cause much harm and embarrassment to all concerned.

The disabled rider approaches and takes his riding lessons very seriously, knowing full well why he is doing them and what is expected of him as a rider. These riders take their spills and knocks, laugh at themselves and their fellow pupils, get annoyed and frustrated just as any perfectly healthy class of riders, but for sheer grit, determination and concentration no instructor will find a more enjoyable, satisfying and thoroughly rewarding, responsive group of pupils. But beware the instructor's foe: frustration.

The act of riding the horse is by itself a very strenuous form of exercise and for some individuals, it is sufficient for them to be led around on the horse, reacting to the movements and maintaining balance and posture.

Before getting the student to perform any exercise, the instructor must first consult with the therapist and determine what is best for a particular individual. This may vary within the class and the instructor must plan accordingly.

The aim of exercises is twofold. Firstly, they should aid the rider in controlling the affected part of the body. Secondly, they should aid the rider in controlling the horse. Specifically, exercises will improve balance, posture, coordination and increase the range of motion. They also reduce spasticity and contractions as well as improving muscle tone. All the senses are heightened and sensation and circulation are improved.

The instructor must analyse each individual rider's needs in relation to the stage of tuition reached and the degree of the disability, bearing in mind that constant re-evaluation is necessary as the rider progresses upto the faster paces.

It has been noted that there is a carry over of the benefits of exercises into the activities of daily living that should be watched for by parents and teachers. Other advantages are a general improvement in health, particularly with those individuals who were inclined to suffer from overweight due to lack of exercise.

The relaxing effect on muscles after strenuous exercise has been found extremely beneficial to those affected by muscle spasms. Therefore, it is necessary to ensure that following a hard exercise session, riders must be allowed

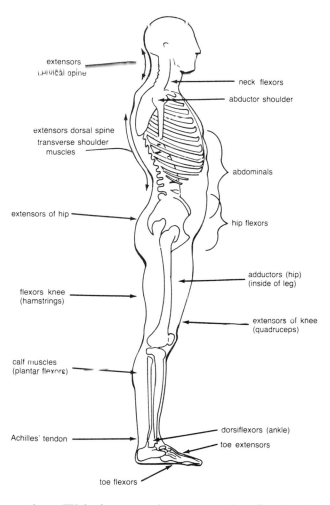

extensors
cervical spine

neck flexors

abductor shoulder

extensors dorsal spine
transverse shoulder
muscles

abdominals

extensors of hip

hip flexors

adductors (hip)
(inside of leg)

flexors knee
(hamstrings)

extensors of knee
(quadruceps)

calf muscles
(plantar flexors)

Achilles' tendon

dorsiflexors (ankle)

toe extensors

toe flexors

Postural groups of muscles. There are two main groups of muscles: flexors – muscles that bend any part of the body or a limb; and extensors – muscles that straighten any part of the body or a limb.

time to relax. This is a good opportunity for the instructor to exercise the senses by asking questions and encouraging a verbal response that will relax the jaw and decrease tension in the neck muscles.

Often with small children in particular, a more energetic response is obtained when exercises are done as part of a game. The response and subsequent benefit is often greater when the individual is unaware of being observed.

To appreciate the basic needs of the individual, the

Groups of muscles.

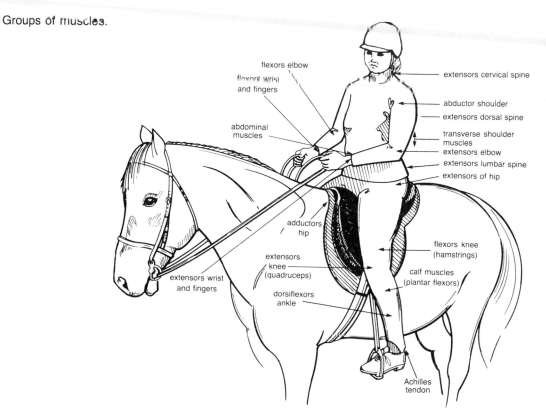

instructor must become familiar with the groups of muscles and their function, when the rider is either standing or seated in the saddle. (See diagrams – page 103 and above.) The exercises that follow are similar to those used in all riding centres. The instructor must learn to adapt them to each individual and lay emphasis on those which are more suitable for each individual in a particular class.

Exercise 1: Touching the Toes

The rider, once seated in the saddle, is made to perform this exercise in one of two different ways. The first method is to bend and touch the toes on the same side as the hand, and the second to reach for the toe on the opposite side, crossing forwards over the pony's shoulder. Both forms benefit the rider equally but, of course, one way is more strenuous and difficult to do than the other. Spastic riders will derive more benefit from the second method rather than the first.

With the hand that is not reaching for the toe placed on the hip bone, so that the rider is discouraged from using it to lower himself, the pupil raises the arm to its fullest extent and then, bending forward from the waist, reaches down to touch the toes, which should be turned up to meet the fingers by bending the ankle joint, without lifting the leg or raising the knee. The instructor should also ensure that the leg on the opposite side remains in the correct position and that the seat does not lift from the saddle.

This exercise strengthens the neck, back and hip muscles, increases close contact of the knee, thigh and ankle joints, resulting in a better balance.

Exercise 2: Forwards Bending

In bending forwards on to the pony's neck the pupil must place both hands on the hips (at first he may be allowed to fold the arms), but there is a tendency, if so allowed, for him to use the arms to lower and lift the trunk instead of using the stomach and back muscles.

The object is to get as low as possible on to the pony's neck bending from the waist, without lifting the seat or losing balance, until the chin touches the pony's mane or crest. The head should be held up, feeling the collar on the back of the neck, while the rider looks ahead between the pony's ears.

This exercise will be found useful later on for demonstrating the forward jumping position. It develops the hip, stomach and back muscles and strengthens the neck.

Forwards bending exercise.

The instructor should make sure that his pupil does not let the toe point down or the leg swing too far back as he bends forwards from the hips. With spastic pupils it is better if the instructor can get them to bend from the hips with the legs kept straight and the feet out of the stirrups, because this will assist in breaking the rigid pattern that is peculiar to this particular group.

Exercise 3: Standing up in the Stirrups

This exercise fulfils two requirements: firstly, it teaches and helps the rider, unless he is a spastic, to keep the lower leg in the correct position; and secondly, it gives him a sense of balance and confidence.

On the command 'Stand up' the rider pushes down on the stirrup iron with the ball of the foot, keeping the heel lower than the toes, straightens the leg from the knee which stays close to the saddle flap or knee roll and lifts the seat pulling it in by bracing the back and stomach muscles.

If the lower leg is allowed to swing back out of line the rider will lose his balance and fall forward on the pony's neck. Alternatively, if the leg points forwards he will find it difficult to stand up and may resort to pulling himself up by using his hands on the front of the saddle. Once clear of the saddle the rider maintains his position like a pendulum, with the lower leg acting as a counter weight against any loss of balance.

This exercise as described will *not* benefit the spastic rider, in fact if done this way it can harm him because it makes him use the muscle spasm in a wrong pattern, which we are trying to avoid and reduce at all costs. If, however, he is required to stand up in the stirrups the instructor should allow him to slide the foot home into the stirrup iron to encourage the downwards pressure of the heel. Also, he must be discouraged from increasing the inwards turn of the knee as he rises, because we are trying to create flexion combined with extension, not inwards pressure which is already sufficient. In medical terms, adduction is not required in these cases.

Exercise 4: 'Around the World'

'Around the world' has become more of a game than an exercise as riders tend to treat it as a lighthearted respite from the more strenuous exercises. It is in fact 'top of the pops' where exercise requests are concerned. In spite of its popularity, however, it is still very demanding on students' physical ability, sense of co-ordination and balance.

It is *not* recommended that this exercise should be attempted by pupils of a nervous disposition as it could easily undo all attempts in the earlier stages of giving confidence.

The exercise itself, as the name implies, entails the rider revolving a complete circle while still sitting on the horse. That is the intention but all too often pupils tend to get carried away and literally spin themselves earthwards with gay abandon, much to the delight of their fellows.

'Around the world' exercise – the point of no return!

Starting with either leg (it does not matter which) the rider raises it in front and lifts it over clear of the mane, at the same time turning in the saddle to face sideways so that both legs are now on the same side. Then lifting the leg nearest to the horse's rear he again swings it over clear of the quarters and at the same time revolves in the saddle until, with the legs either side of the horse, he faces out over the 'stern' end! Obviously he cannot be left in this precarious position for long, so the movement is continued with alternate legs spinning over, until he is once again facing in the right direction.

Pupils may be allowed at first to hold on to the front or back of the saddle to help keep their balance, but eventually the exercise should be done with folded arms.

Besides being great fun this exercise benefits riders physically and mentally because when introduced as a race it sets up the competitive spirit so essential when trying to get them to respond.

Exercise 5: Clapping Heels in Front and Behind

These two exercises in one form a curtain-raiser or rehearsal for 'Around the World', as the rider is asked to clap the heels together both in front and behind the saddle. To clap in front, he rests both hands on the pony's quarters behind the saddle and lifts the legs up in front, clapping the heels together above the mane before returning them back to the correct position.

Clapping behind is done by resting both hands either side of the withers and lifting the body clear of the saddle and pony as in a vault. As the highest point of lift is reached he claps the heels behind well above the pony's quarters. The legs should not be allowed to bend at the knees either on the forward or backward movements.

These exercises develop the arms, legs and trunk as well

as giving the pupil confidence in himself and his pony.

Ponies must obviously be well rehearsed at this exercise, by a groom or the instructor, to ensure that they do not object to the sudden noise and movement. The leader holding the pony can assist on the forward clap by keeping the pony's head held down. This will also avoid the risk of the pony's mane, or worse his ears, being caught between the rider's heels.

Pupils suffering from cerebral palsy or any form of spasticity should *not* be allowed to attempt the forward clap as this will again encourage the spasmodic pattern. The backward movement can, however, be used to good effect so long as the knees are kept straight.

Exercise 6: Foot and Leg Exercises

These exercises have proved to be of benefit to spastic pupils in particular, as they supple and relax the ankle joint, which eventually makes it easier for them to walk correctly with the heel firmly down on the ground. The amount of improvement is noticeable in some cases even after only a few months of riding.

While doing this particular exercise the instructor must ensure that his pupil does not bend forwards or look down at the feet. At first, riders tend to favour one particular side, working harder on one leg than the other, so the instructor must ensure that both sides are worked equally, with concentration on the leg that needs improving.

Sitting upright in the saddle the pupil is asked to circle and lift the foot from the ankle joint, firstly towards the horse and then away. It will help if the instructor tells him to imagine he is holding a piece of chalk between the toes with which to draw as large a circle as possible on an imaginary blackboard. While doing so he must neither allow the knee to drift away from the saddle nor the leg to lift.

Another exercise, which strengthens the hamstrings and

the muscles in the calf, is swinging the leg either forwards and backwards or pushing them out from the horse's side as far as they will go. The latter will also stretch and develop the inner thigh muscles. Both of these exercises must be done keeping the toes up and pointing to the front.

Any pupil who has a pinned or fused joint or any condition similar to arthritis in the joint must not attempt any violent exercises which would aggravate the condition in those areas.

Exercise 7: Circling Arms and Hands

This exercise can be divided into individual movements or it can be done as a complete routine. The riders again raise their arms at right angles to the body with fingers outstretched and palms facing down. Starting with the hands, they should begin to circle them forwards from the wrist joint, keeping the arms straight without bending from the elbow or shoulder.

After a few moments of circling forwards the process is reversed and the hands are circled in the opposite direction. This ensures that the wrists are relaxed and supple as well as strengthening the forearm, which will eventually help to give the pupils the ability to 'feel' the pony's mouth through the reins, without having stiff or rigid hands and wrists.

The instructor can stop the exercise at this point, let his pupils relax for a while and then ask them to raise the arms again and circle them from the shoulder. Alternatively, he can continue from the wrist movement to enlarge the circle gradually, until the whole arm is revolving in increasing sweeps, above the head and down past the horse's flanks from the shoulder joints.

During the whole time that arm exercises are being done, the instructor must make sure that the rider's seat and leg position do not alter. With a rider afflicted by cerebral palsy it is better if the instructor asks him to commence this movement from the shoulder end and work down towards the hands while the palms face upwards.

Exercise 8: Trunk Twisting (Arms Extended)

Arm exercises are particularly beneficial to pupils who suffer from muscular weakness following poliomyelitis, and the exercises involving raising, circling and stretching of the arms have produced excellent results in muscular improvement.

Twisting from the waist with arms extended teaches the rider to sit deep and maintain a firm balance. It also strengthens and supples the abdominal and back muscles as well as the shoulders and arms.

Both arms should be raised out sideways with the palms facing downwards and fingers outstretched, level with the shoulders. With spastic pupils the palms should face up or forwards, not down. On the command 'Turn', the rider turns the top half of the body from the waist first to the left, back to face the front and then to the right. The movement is continued smoothly for as long as the instructor considers sufficient. The arms must be kept out at right angles to the body the whole time, while the pupil faces in the direction of the turn without turning the head beyond the line of the body.

Exercise 9: 'Do as I Say'

As with 'Around the world' this exercise has become more of a game, as the riders try to keep up with the instructor without realising the actual physical work involved.

The instructor informs the class that he wants them to do as he says and not as he does. He then goes through the process of placing his hands on the hips, shoulders, head and then straight up in the air. As he does so he shouts out a different command to what he is actually doing. For instance as he places his hands on his hips he says, 'Hands on head'. The riders must quickly follow his verbal commands while watching him the whole time.

After a while some pupils may get crafty and close their eyes to avoid being distracted, so the instructor must make sure that all eyes are on him. As well as the physical good it does the riders, the exercise also increases their powers of observation and concentration.

Exercise 10: Lying Back on the Quarters

Even to an able-bodied rider this exercise presents difficulties but to the spastic pupil lying back on the quarters can be a very painful experience at first, because of the difficulty of being able to straighten the body and legs.

Lying back on the quarters.

Therefore, care should be taken to ensure that the movement is gradually built up over a period of time, until the rider is capable of completing it without pain or injury. Nonetheless, it does and will benefit him a great deal if performed correctly, so the instructor should persevere with friendly persuasion towards the ultimate goal.

The object is to lie back over the cantle of the saddle until the shoulders and head are resting on the pony's quarters. To do so the pupil should remove both feet from the stirrups and then fold the arms, as there is a temptation to hang on to the front of the saddle or reins. Looking straight ahead or at the pony's ears he then slowly lowers back until his shoulders touch the quarters, allowing the head to rest finally just above the top of the tail.

Riders must be made to concentrate on keeping the legs, from the knees downwards, lying against the horse's side in the correct position without allowing them to swing forwards and up. Haste in going down and in rising should be avoided, as one of the main reasons for this exercise is to strengthen the stomach muscles. The slower it is done the better. Other parts of the body that will benefit are the neck, loins, and leg muscles.

The exercises I have described are a small selection of a far greater number that an experienced and inventive instructor can think up, and the more variety and humour that can be put into them the less likely pupils are to become bored and subsequently lazy, and the more likely they are to become proficient riders. Whatever the exercise, however, the instructor must ensure, particularly with spastic pupils, that they do not attempt to do them too fast, as this can lead to a return of muscle spasm and cramp.

With pupils suffering from post-poliomyelitis, amputees and some paraplegics, the effect of rushing the exercises is not so noticeable, in fact the momentum gained can assist them, but it is better if the instructor does make his pupils, regardless of their disabilities, perform them slowly at first and gradually build up the speed where necessary, with frequent consultations with the physiotherapist as to the pupil's physical progress and the type of exercise best suited for the particular disability.

Frustration

Everyone who rides is aware of the problem of inner frustration, caused by aggravation at one's own inability to accomplish something, whether it's a certain movement that one never seems able to get right, the horse failing to respond or just not being placed well in a particular class.

In all sports, frustration is constantly present and continually has to be recognised and overcome if progress is to be made. In a handicapped programme, instructors, riders and even volunteers, to a certain extent, experience the feeling frequently and perhaps for lengthy periods of time.

The rider who is mentally aware of how something should be done but physically experiences difficulty at every stage of learning, probably suffers more from frustration than most.

The instructor who wants the student to progress and yet can see the difficulties also experiences the feeling to a lesser degree, while the volunteer, leader or side helper, who inevitably forms an association with the student, feels for his charge and is therefore tempted to over-assist merely as a result of good intentions.

In all cases, if the feeling is allowed to persist, it can lead to surrender and abdication of responsibility, which can lead to depression. There are various ways of avoiding or alleviating this problem, all of which will be of benefit to rider, instructor and helper.

The introduction of games and competitive exercises into lessons will accomplish two aims. Firstly, it will invariably show up the rider's true ability, because when students are unaware that they are being observed, they often perform with far more enthusiasm than when working under individual supervision which can cause self-consciousness. Secondly, the incentive of games or competitions will often make the rider put forth more effort or use an alternative or compensating method to attain the desired goal.

The excitement and risk of games and competitions that are within the mental and physical capabilities of each student will increase the desire to participate and consequently make the student more aware through an increased circulation of adrenalin that boosts muscle tone and coordination. Consultation with the therapist will determine which students are capable of sudden or prolonged sessions of excitement or risk exercise.

Obviously, those riders who are under sedation for such things as hyperactivity or mental stress should be approached differently.

Regardless of the type of games or competition, and there are many that are suitable (see chapter on games), the instructor should begin with the simpler ones and build up the degree of difficulty and excitement involved. It is important that the games chosen are ones that can be readily understood and done reasonably well by the individual student.

During a specific lesson, game or exercise, if the rider experiences difficulty or shows signs of frustration after trying for a few times, the instructor can allow, or in fact encourage the use of compensating aids or try another method of accomplishing the same goal (see chapter on the aids).

Inventiveness and compromise will help and the instructor can always jump ahead and step up the learning process and go back, if necessary, another time for repetition.

It is helpful also if the instructor looks for an exercise which the rider finds easy, and use that as a reward, giving much praise and encouragement when the student attempts something that is difficult. Instructors should not dwell too long on any movement or exercise that may cause aggravation and subsequent frustration

A frequent change of horse where possible, and a change of leader or side helper, will often create a new situation that will initiate a revitalisation of effort and interest.

It is imperative that the instructor and volunteers never make the student aware of any frustration they themselves may experience, in their desire to see the rider progress.

The whole learning process, in most cases, is painfully slow and this is one of the reasons why the instructor of the disabled in horseback riding requires such a highly qualified and experienced approach.

8 The Paces

In the last chapter I described the beneficial effect of exercises in developing the rider's seat and back muscles. When we reach the point where we begin to teach the student how to use the seat in making the horse move forward and to halt, the benefit derived from the exercises will become apparent.

The most important and naturally applied aid that a rider possesses is the seat, or body weight, that is used by the action of bracing the back and driving downwards and forwards. By bracing I do not mean hollowing, as this would tend to have the opposite effect from that which is required to propel the horse forwards.

With certain disabilities, namely post-polio or paraplegics versus cerebral palsy or stroke victims, we have to approach the method of getting them to apply the aids, and in fact, to ride, from different angles because of the vast difference in the effect of the various disabilities.

When a pupil is affected by muscular wastage or lack of sensation in the lower limbs, it is absolutely useless to expect them ever to possess a sufficient degree of strength or control over their limbs, or whatever part of their body is affected, to be capable of applying the correct legs aids sufficiently clearly for the horse to obey without being confused. Muscles that have deteriorated will not miraculously appear again, regardless of what exercise or form of therapy is used. The best we can hope for is very slight improvements in coordination, control and, over a period of time, minute improvements in tone and usage.

Other muscles not affected, however, can be trained to take their place and be encouraged to perform a task that is not normally required of them. Similarly, other healthy parts of the body can compensate and be used to a greater degree than would normally be so, if it were not for the weakness. This does not mean, however, that what little powers of strength or control the particular student has should not be encouraged to be used to their maximum possible capability. The compensating factor should merely be a temporary stop-gap wherever possible.

A rider whose legs are affected by this muscular wastage or lack of sensation has very little control over them and it is sufficient to expect those students to keep the legs reasonably still at the horse's sides and in the stirrups. The upper torso, however, once the rider has acquired good balance and is not dependent on the hands to achieve it, can be used very effectively in influencing the horse's paces.

Other students, such as the cerebral palsy athetoid or spastic, may experience difficulties with coordination of movements and control of the limbs plus an over-abundance of strength which they must learn to control. The emphasis for these students must be for the instructor to initially concentrate on the rider's balance in rhythm with the horse and the ability to follow the forward movement by the action, or driving influence, of the seat and back. With this in mind, the instructor can begin to explain the aids, remembering, of course, not to leave anything out because even though a rider may not be actually capable of doing it, they are capable of absorbing mentally the theoretical knowledge which will be of valuable assistance later. Knowing *how* to do something is half the battle won.

To obtain a good balance it is essential for the rider to have a knowledge of and experience all the paces in their proper order. Exercises at the halt on a variety of ponies and horses will have developed a feel for the width and height. Theoretically, students must be made aware of the correct sequence of the horse's movement for all paces. Practical demonstrations by the instructor will help in this understanding.

The walk, with its steady four-beat rhythm is probably

the pace that will be experienced by the student more than any other. With leaders and helpers and later without assist-ance, the student will learn to adapt to the steady rhythmic movement forwards, sideways and up. Constant re adjust-ment is necessary, particularly when the horse is moving, to maintain balance. The slow continual massaging effect of the walk will help develop balance, feel and confidence more than any other pace.

It is important that leaders encourage the horses to main-tain a good walk and not allow them to drop into a lazy shuffle. Leaders also should be careful of sharp turns that can cause the rider a balance problem. Over-assistance by helpers at the walk can be detrimental to riders who must learn to adjust to a loss of balance and recover by their own ability.

The two-beat rhythm of the trot with the subsequent bouncing out of the saddle, is to some disabled riders, very difficult to become accustomed to. It is important that, as far as possible within the limited number of horses available, ponies with a good regular, comfortable trot should be used for first-time trotters.

The sitting trot to some students, such as the cerebral palsy spastic and the athetoid, can be a bone-jarring experi-ence. It has been noticed that these two disabilities and others similarly affected, find the rising or posting trot easier to accomplish. Amputees, paraplegics and others with lower weaknesses, however, find the sitting position easier and rising, owing to the lack of strength in the legs, very diffi-cult. For both groups to be capable of rising, the long hand hold, or a good handful of mane in the beginning stages is an advantage.

The relaxing effect of the 'shake-up' in the trot to spastic muscles, once the transition to the walk is made, is very noticeable. The athetoid also sits much more quietly following a period of trotting. This proves that if muscles and joints are made to work hard enough, they will benefit from the relaxation that follows.

Riders with spinal deformities and hemiplegics should be observed carefully from behind by the instructor when they post to the trot, to ensure they rise equally from both sides and do not twist or favour the strong side. Should the rider sit or post continually one-sided it could result in a curvature of the spine. This applies, though on a limited scale, to all paces.

Helpers are, of course, essential for the first trotting lesson to preserve balance and instil confidence. They should be well rehearsed on how to assist the rider at this particular time and not over-assist.

The canter, undertaken on a smooth-gaited animal capable of maintaining a good three-beat rhythm with the hocks well under, is not an uncomfortable pace for disabled students. Providing the lift in the period of suspension is not too high, riders find little difficulty in maintaining balance and posture. A horse that reverts to a four-beat canter is not to be tolerated, even though it may be comfortable for the rider, as it gives a false impression of the desired pace.

In the early stages of teaching the canter, the horse can be lunged, with the rider using the handles of a standard vaulting surcingle and a pad, until the student becomes proficient enough to ride alone.

For riding out, horses can be trained to walk, trot, and canter while being led from another horse.

Once the rider is accomplished at the three standard paces, he will find little difficulty in moving the horse up into a gallop if and when he feels the urge. Being carried along on the faster four-beat rhythm again should not cause any real difficulty to the student who has reached this stage.

The basics of dressage, introducing lateral movements, and jumping are within the reach of many disabled riders who should be allowed the right to choose their own goals and encouraged to perform to their maximum potential.

9 The Aids

Before describing the correct aids for the basic paces and movements, I will first explain some of the problems the instructor must expect and will encounter when teaching a disabled pupil how to apply them.

It will be noticed immediately, by virtue of their importance in riding, that the legs in particular are generally affected. Many riders experience great difficulty in stretching the knees apart, or extending the legs down the horse's sides into the position required for a good contact and a clear application. A student whose legs are affected by muscle spasm or exaggerated stiffness will find it practically impossible to keep the toes up and the heels down, with the foot correctly resting on the stirrup iron. This in turn makes it very difficult for the leg to extend or be flexible enough for the rider to be capable of transferring intentions through the leg aids to the horse. Uncontrolled athetoid movement in the muscles and joints also make it extremely difficult to keep the legs still, creating a false aid or an exaggerated signal at the wrong moment. Other riders, such as postpolio, paraplegic or spina bifida students, find that the lack of power or the inability to feel or control the lower legs makes the application of the leg aids almost impossible.

In many cases, nature, with a little therapeutic help, has given these pupils a physically improved torso which can be used to compensate for weakness to a certain degree.

The cerebral palsy spastic or athetoid students, however, are not so fortunate, as the whole body and arms may also be affected by spasm and rigidity.

In these instances the instructor must, through suppling exercises and by utilising the movement of the horse, concentrate on teaching the pupils to relax the tensions in the affected areas, so that by the time the students have reached the stage of riding alone they are capable of getting some degree of control and obedience from their applied aids. The harder and more vigorously the muscles are made to work, in a planned systematic progressive pattern, the more noticeably and quickly the muscles will relax and thereby benefit.

From then on, time, patience and perseverance are both the instructor's and the pupil's closest allies.

The natural aids the rider possesses are the seat, in conjunction with body weight, the legs, hands and voice, in order of priority. The instructor must determine which must be developed or concentrated upon if any one of them is to be discounted because of the student's disability. Provided the rider is capable of using the correct aids, however limited, then the lesson is straightforward and should be taught in the normal way. If compensation is to be allowed or encouraged, either temporarily or permanently, the instructor and therapist should discuss what form this should take.

Compensating aids are the means by which the rider uses, or develops for use, a stronger or fitter part of the body, or a limb to take over, or assist a weaker or less effective part. There are instances where this can effectively assist the rider but sometimes, to allow such compensations would be detrimental to the rider and to progress. Close liaison with the therapist is therefore essential at all advancing stages. Examples of some obvious compensating aids are firstly the exaggerated use of the seat and back to provide forward impulsion, in the event of weakness in the lower limbs. Some riders have a naturally over-developed upper torso which makes this possible, but they must be carefully observed from behind, to ensure that the thrust is equal on both sides and that no twisting of the hips or spine occurs, which could cause a scoliosis or undue strain on the spine. Post-polio riders and some paraplegics find this method makes up for the lack of power in the legs.

The riding stick or dressage schooling whip used in conjunction with the action of the back and seat also adds to the effectiveness of the aids, provided the rider is instructed regarding the correct use.

The voice plays a much greater role as an aid and should be allowed by the instructor far more often then would be permitted in a normal class of students. A sharp 'walk on!' or a gentle 'whoa', for instance, can produce good results from a horse that has been trained to respond to the voice.

Some disabilities should not be permitted to use compensation merely to make it easier. The hemiplegic, for example, affected on one side, must be encouraged to use the weaker limb wherever possible.

If there is a possibility of improved muscle tone or joint mobility the student must be made to work at it and use the correct signal. To avoid the risk of frustration, however, compensation should be allowed if extreme difficulty is experienced.

No two riders are alike and no two disabilities affect the student in exactly the same way. It is up to the instructor and therapist to determine how to obtain maximum efficiency and self-help from each individual. A constant re-evaluation and adjustment of methods is necessary. The ultimate aim is to encourage the rider to become capable of relaying his intentions and receiving a response to his signals, however unorthodox the aids may be.

Before allowing the use of any artificial aids such as the stick, instructors should determine the rider's ability to control its movement and only allow minimal use to emphasise the normal aids. Spurs are not recommended for use by disabled riders, other than by those whose disability is so minimal that it allows almost normal function of the legs.

Callipers or braces, either short or long, worn on the legs, should be removed whenever possible when riding. Not only do they cause holes in the clothing where sharp edges protude, but they also restrict contact or feel of the horse and make movement of the rider's legs difficult. The rough ends of bolts or hinges touching the horse's side are (to the horse) similar to the touch of the spur and can produce unwanted and sudden reactions.

Before attempting to ask the horse to move forward the rider must first of all get his attention, so that the horse is alert and will be responsive to his demands. This process is known in riding as 'collection' and it simply means the gathering together under the rider's seat and in his hands of as much of the horse's power and energy as he needs, at the instance and in the amount required for a particular pace or movement.

The rider having spent some considerable time on the leading rein or on the lunge, should have learnt to feel this energy through the movement of the horse, particularly from the drive of the hindquarters. Now on his own he must acquire the sensations and learn the method of drawing upon and harnessing this energy, by this series of signals called the 'aids'.

Sitting firmly down into the centre of the saddle in the balanced seat position, he takes up the reins, making sure that they are of an equal length and not twisted. Keeping the hands in the correct position already described, he then shortens the reins until he has an elastic contact or 'feel' on the bit in the pony's mouth. This will tell the pony that more is to follow and he should signify his response (whether it be delightful expectancy or not) by a backward movement of the ears and by raising the head. The swishing of the tail must not be confused with 'delightful expectancy' but perhaps more as a sign of impatience or annoyance at the rider's indecision. The pupil must know how, where and what he is going to do before attempting to do it. If he does not know he should not try it, because if the horse does not react, or does react too violently, very often the blame is laid on the wrong doorstep.

At this stage, however, having merely taken up the reins, the response may be a little uncertain and apprehensive, so the rider must now proceed to make the message clear.

By bracing the back muscles and driving the seat bones downwards and forwards into the saddle, as if trying to propel the horse from under him and at the same time closing the lower legs firmly against the horse's sides, just behind the girth, again by a downwards and forwards squeeze, he will encourage the horse to close up by drawing his hind legs underneath his quarters. The rider, through his seat, should now feel the hocks bend under and the back lift slightly as the horse closes up into his hands. As the seat and legs are applied the rider must maintain a firm but flexible feel on the reins to prevent the horse moving forward and also contain the energy he has created, while keeping an upright but relaxed position looking straight ahead. The horse should now be attentive and perfectly balanced, ready to obey his rider's next command to walk on. Throughout the whole process leaders and side walkers should be ready to assist, in the event of difficulty or disobedience, without over-assisting or taking over because of impatience.

The Walk

Employing the same tactics as for the collection, the pupil again drives in and forwards with the seat and at the same time applying both legs again just behind the girth. Depending on the type and temperament of the animal, and the extent of his education or schooling, the rider learns to adjust the strength of the leg aids. Often a firm squeeze of the lower inside leg is sufficient, but a stronger aid may be needed for a lazy or heavier type of horse, in which case the heel can be applied also low down should it be considered necessary. As the seat and legs are used the pupil this time gives or relaxes the tension on the reins, by opening the curved fingers slightly, to allow the horse to move forward and accept the bit.

Once the horse is walking on with a firm four-beat rhythm, he must endeavour to follow the movement by the action of the back and seat, keeping the legs close to the girth to be able to continually maintain the forward impulsion drawn from behind. The hands, resting above and in front of the saddle, and the width of the pony's mouth apart, should maintain an even feel on the bit without restricting the necessary action of the head and neck.

With the horse and pupil moving forward at a collected walk, the instructor can now use all the normal riding school movements such as turns, circles, changes or rein, etc., at the walk, teaching the rider to apply the correct diagonal aids where he is capable of doing so, once again bearing in mind each individual disability, with much emphasis laid on the use of the seat.

After the horse has been put through various collected movements for any length of time the instructor should allow both horse and rider to relax.

By letting the rein out to a good length, a process known as walking with a 'free' rein, the rider allows the horse to stretch the head and neck out or down to rest the neck muscles. At the same time keeping the horse moving forwards from the seat, he eases the pressure of the legs and lets the horse resort back to a relaxed stroll until he is required to be attentive again before the next movement.

The Halt

Before a rider can actually bring a horse to a halt he must again warn him of his intention by collection, in the form of a half-halt or pause in the rhythmic cadence. By driving forwards with the seat and applying the legs the rider closes the horse up under the saddle, this time into restraining hands. As the horse feels the pressure on the bit and slows to a collected halt, the rider relaxes the hands and leg pressure, letting the seat sink into the centre of the saddle.

During the whole operation of halting, the rider's body must not be allowed to deviate either forwards or backwards from the vertical line, neither should the legs swing or increase the forwards pressure on the stirrup irons.

The horse should be made to stand with all four feet firmly on the ground, with the hocks bent under and the head erect with a relaxed lower jaw.

The Trot

Sitting Trot. The trot, a pace at which the horse changes the rhythm of the cadence from four beats to two diagonals alternating, is an excellent pace for working or shaking the rider down into the saddle. Provided the rider learns to relax and absorb the more exaggerated throw up through his seat and back muscles, it need not be as tiring or jarring to the rider as it may at first appear or feel.

For spastic pupils the relaxed position takes longer to acquire and the instructor must work at it; but polio sufferers, paraplegics and the like fall more naturally into the desired state of body control.

Because of the more pronounced free forward action of the trot the rider must learn to adjust the angle of the body slightly to move with the horse and not be left behind the movement, at the same time retaining the position and depth of his seat. With disabled riders, who are so dependent on balance, the more firmly entrenched we can get them into the saddle the less likely they are to part company with it and the sitting trot can and is being used to great advantage to this end.

Before expecting his pupil to be capable of this relaxed position the instructor should let him feel the different movement through his seat from the drive behind, without allowing him to resort to using the reins as a means of support. The horse at this stage of learning should always be led by a knowledgeable assistant, or if possible put on the lunge.

So that the rider does not succumb to the temptation of

'hanging-on', the neck strap or D-strap may be used in the early stages to assist the pupil to draw himself down.

When the pupil is capable of maintaining a firm seat without any loss of balance, and is able to apply whatever aids he possesses sufficiently clearly for the horse to understand, we can then dispense with the services of the leaders or helpers (temporarily of course) and begin to teach him to drive the horse into the trot and maintain a fluid, even pace on his own.

To obtain the necessary impetus the rider closes the horse up into his hands in the manner already described, bringing the horse into a collected half-halt before applying the aids to send him forwards smoothly into the transition. The aids, similar to those used in making the horse walk on, entail the use of the seat and back muscles combined with equal leg pressure behind the girth.

As the horse moves forward at the new pace the rider relaxes the feel on the mouth, taking up the contact again once the desired degree of impulsion is obtained.

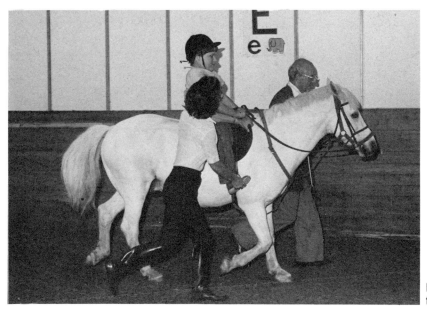

Learning to master the sitting trot.

The Rising Trot. In the majority of riding schools pupils are taught, and quite rightly so, to use the movement of the horse to assist them in rising or 'posting' to the trot and not to lay too much emphasis on the use of the leg or foot on the stirrup iron. It is often taught that if the rider attempts to lift the body too high, by straightening the leg at the knee joint, he may lose the contact of the knee and thigh and consequently his balance. This is of course correct but it is obvious to anyone who has tried the rising trot that a certain amount of leg and knee pressure is required to assist the rider to lift up and forwards.

With pupils whose legs are affected by poliomyelitis up to the waist, or amputees, it is virtually impossible for them to accomplish this movement, unless they resort to the use of the hands to push themselves up or possess extraordinarily well-developed stomach muscles. Even with a physically strengthened abdomen the rider tends merely to thrust the stomach out or lift the body too straight and he is thereby left behind the forward movement or becomes one-sided in his balance.

This being the case it must be obvious to the instructor that the process of rising to the trot, as far as these particular pupils are concerned, is best left alone, other than explaining its benefits to a capable rider.

Spastic pupils and others similarly affected, once they have overcome the stiffness and rigidity in their muscles, can generally be taught to rise to the trot and in fact find it far easier than to remain sitting for any length of time. If they are made to sit at this more extended movement for long periods there is a risk of tension returning which will result in a forced cramped position once again.

To rise correctly the pupil must feel the rhythm of the diagonals and may be allowed at first to glance down at the horse's shoulder to determine the correct leg. The instructor should of course demonstrate and explain the degrees of paces to his class before commencing the lesson.

The metronomic rhythm varies according to the size or

type of pony and the pupil should be given every opportunity to practise posting on different mounts, so that he learns to adjust the height and speed of his rising according to the movement of the horse. In unison with the alternate diagonal he rises from the saddle, using the knees as the pivot point and the thigh muscles to lift as the fore leg on the same side as the direction the horse is moving in comes forward and strikes the ground.

This impetus of the horse will also assist in throwing the rider up and the pupil must be taught to utilise it to his own advantage. Should the seat be thrown or raised too high out of the saddle he may miss a beat and lose his cohesion.

The body should be inclined forwards at approximately forty-five degrees over the hands, which must be kept low and still while maintaining a contact on the horse's mouth. On no account must the rider look down or round the back, as this would tend to throw the weight on to the forehand, causing a loss of balance. The position of the lower leg should be maintained close behind the girth, without allowing it to swing forwards or backwards.

Before attempting to rise, the horse must be made to move on at a medium trot and if there is any loss of impulsion and the rider finds himself rising in slow motion he should return to sitting trot again and apply the aids to increase the drive. For this reason, also, any increase or decrease of pace and changes of direction must be done from the sitting position.

The Canter

With the exception of the walk, the canter is perhaps the most comfortable pace at which disabled pupils can sit, once they have acquired a reasonably relaxed and secure position.

As with the transition from walk to trot the horse changes the rhythm of his pace, this time into three distinct beats. A canter stride commences with the hind leg opposite the leading fore leg, followed by the diagonal pair and then the

School movements.

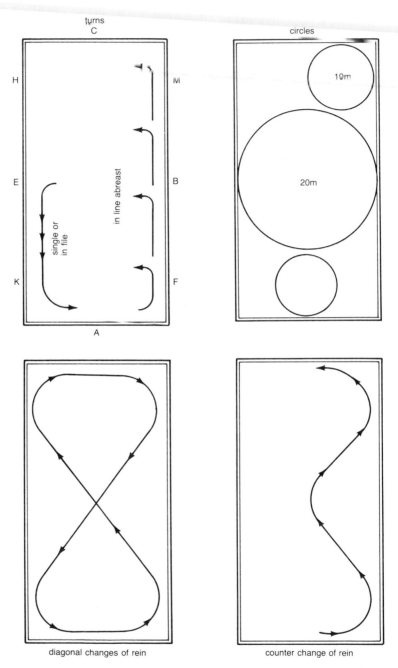

turn and change

reverse changes

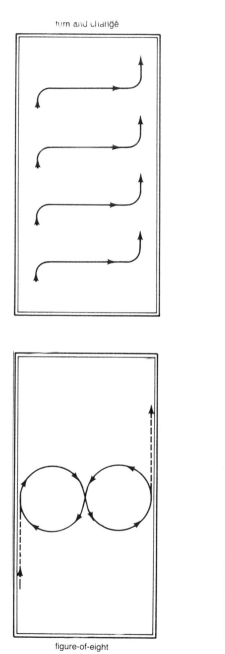
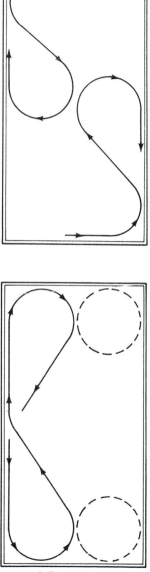

figure-of-eight

half and full voltes

leading fore leg. There is in actual fact a further beat, or period of suspension, when all four legs are off the ground for a split second.

Provided the rider has progressed satisfactorily through the other two stages and is able to apply the aids clearly and smoothly to the best of his ability, there is no reason why the canter should not be taught. In fact the difficulty lies in preventing riders from attempting this pace too early, as they find the smoother rocking action of a collected canter far easier to accomplish and relax into than the more jerky movement of the trot.

Every rider knows that the ultimate aim is to make the change into the canter eventually from the walk, as this is to the horse a more natural transition. However, even the best of riders find it difficult to be able to apply the aids clearly enough to accomplish this; generally they move up into and down from the canter at first from a collected sitting trot. Disabled riders, who can seldom hope to possess sufficient control over the horse to be able to demand this high degree of collection and impulsion, are therefore taught to canter, following and returning to the sitting trot.

This being the first lesson of a new pace they should be provided with a neck strap to reach for in case of loss of balance.

The leaders, who until now have accompanied the rider, are not required for this movement because, firstly, to try to run with a horse at the canter is something of an endurance test and, secondly, if the rider is insecure or has insufficient control of his body then he should not be asked, and is not yet ready, to attempt this movement. Once again lungeing can be used as an introduction to the new pace.

From the sitting position the pupil brings the horse back into a collected trot as he approaches a corner of the school. From a corner the horse is more likely to strike off with the correct leading leg, as he is naturally flexed in that direction. Taking a slightly stronger feel on the inside rein, which will assist the horse to bend, while maintaining contact with the outside or supporting rein, the rider closes the horse up into the hands by the action of the seat and inside leg on the girth.

At the point where the horse is asked to strike off, he applies the outside leg (that is the leg on the opposite side to which he is moving) behind the girth. This leg action signifies to the horse which leg the rider wishes to commence the canter with and also prevents the quarters from swinging out of line. As the leg is applied the back and seat are used in unison to drive forwards into the first lifting stride. The rider must then relax the fingers to initiate a smooth passage forwards, resuming contact again as the required degree of momentum is obtained.

Once the horse is cantering on smoothly the rider should maintain the impulsion without allowing his body to swing either forwards or backwards. With both legs close to the girth the pupil should endeavour to keep the horse moving on a single track, while holding the correct bend in the required direction.

The canter should flow smoothly without any sign of stiffness on the rider's part or any attempt to pull or rush from the horse. If done correctly, with a relaxed rider, it is a pace which can be continued for some distance without the pupil or horse getting over-tired.

To make the transition back from a canter to the trot or from the trot to the walk, the rider follows the usual pattern of driving forwards into restraining hands, which should give as the horse alters the rhythm, to allow him to make the change smoothly. Whether the intention is to go on into a rising trot or slow to a walk, the rider should remain seated.

10 Jumping

'Nothing ventured, nothing gained' is a very true saying, and it applies well when we are considering whether or not we should take the risk of teaching disabled riders to jump. Despite what has been written and stated by far more knowledgeable persons on the subject, jumping does, in my opinion, entail an element of risk and I make no apologies for using the word. Anyone who takes up show jumping, for instance, will know that it takes nerve, intelligence, quick thinking and a certain devil-may-care attitude, and a slip at the wrong moment can mean disaster.

At no other time during his riding career is a pupil more likely to take a fall; it is unpleasant but inevitable and we must accept the fact that it will happen. Until now we have taken great pains to avoid falls and we must still do so but let us dispense with the cottonwool. If the rider has not progressed satisfactorily by now to be capable of jumping, what is he doing on this lesson?

As a sport, show jumping has, since it was first included in the Olympic Games in 1912, reached great heights in popularity, particularly since competitions have been televised and well-known personalities have been copied, criticised and idolised by thousands of budding equestrians, eager to taste the thrills and excitement of great events.

Disabled riders know that this to them must remain a dream but it will not and does not stop them or us from using jumping as a means to an end. In no other form of riding, except perhaps higher level dressage, is so much demanded or expected either from the horse or rider both physically and mentally.

The risks having been explained, appreciated and accepted by all concerned, we can begin the lesson, knowing full well the pupils' capabilities and that this is perhaps the one day they have looked forward to after months or years of working on the flat, a route many able-bodied riders would do well to follow. It is also proof that they have themselves, by their own perseverance and courage, reached the stage where they have improved sufficiently and have enough confidence in their ability and in their instructor (and he in them) to take this tremendous stride forward.

I do not propose to explain in detail the finer points in teaching a pupil how to jump, as there are numerous excellent books written by experts on the subject and many instructors have their own particular methods. Therefore, I shall merely describe the manner in which we at Chigwell tackled the problem and point out the various complications that can be expected.

When the instructor is satisfied that his pupil has a secure balance and can control the horse at all paces, including the simple change of leg at the canter, he can then begin the jumping lesson. Before commencing, however, he must ensure that all horses and ponies being used are equipped with neck straps and that he has two intelligent and nimble assistants to help in moving and laying out poles and cavaletti.

The ideal place for this first attempt is the indoor school, provided it has a firm, well-laid surface. Horses are less inclined to rush their fences indoors and, being a smaller area, the instructor can cope far more easily than when out in a large paddock.

The surface-covering of an indoor riding school consists usually of a mixture of sand and agricultural salt, mixed perhaps with wood shavings to give buoyancy. Wealthier establishments may even have a floor-covering of tan or peat moss. All these surfaces provide a reasonably soft landing should the rider take a fall but they are harder for the horse to work in as the mixtures do not give such a good spring-assisted take-off as does a well-laid turfed arena . . . but we must progress to that later.

Round rustic logs, old railway sleepers or sawn-off tele-
graph poles are useful starters for introducing horse and
rider to 'picking their way' but they are inclined to be
cumbersome and too heavy to move quickly around the
arena, so are better left out in the grass paddock as 'natural
fences' for use at a later stage. However, it is useless to ask
a horse and rider to learn to jump over matchsticks of poles
that will either break at the first touch of a hoof or be sent
flying and become tangled between the horse's legs should
he be clumsy enough to trip over them.

It is obvious, therefore, that we must find something that
is both light enough to move quickly and yet solid enough
to let the horse know he must clear it by stepping or jumping
over.

Cavaletti, which do not tip easily and are generally used
to teach able-bodied riders to jump, are not recommended,
except for students who, by nature of their improved ability,
or lesser disability, are capable of jumping.

Those who require either a leader or side helper should
start with poles, either on the ground or positioned at correct
distances on blocks, to avoid the risk of horse or helper
tripping or knocking their shins, which could cause a threat
to safety.

Once they have progressed to riding unassisted, students
may then consider the use of cavaletti and other more chal-
lenging obstacles.

The benefit the horse derives from being worked over
calvaletti and poles is threefold. It teaches him to look where
he is putting his feet and, in so doing, lower the head,
thereby strengthening the neck muscles; it also deters him
from going too fast.

To the rider it teaches balance in unison with the lifting
and lowering action, 'feel' through the reins, following the
movement of the horse's head and confidence in his ability.

Starting with a single obstacle we ask the rider, who has
previously warmed up himself and his pony with a few
suppling exercises and movements, to approach the pole,

which is laid on the ground or set at a very low height, from the long side of the school at the collected trot. The method of approach is very important at this stage and the pupil must endeavour to keep the horse central to the pole, at the same time maintaining the forward impulsion without any attempt to rush.

As the horse travels over the jump the pupil's hands and body should follow the action of the head and neck; if necessary the neck strap can be held for support in preference to the reins, but it is better if the pupil can learn to 'give' with the movement by anticipating slightly without having to resort to clinging on. After the jump the horse should be taken in hand again as smoothly as possible and driven straight on without any attempt at slowing down. The rider must never turn to look back at the jump as he returns to the saddle on landing.

From now on the instructor can increase the height, add more jumps and vary the number and distance of the poles, using the whole of the arena to give multiple changes of direction as the rider progresses. For the approach at the trot, six poles can be spaced out at between 4 and 5 feet distance, and for the canter at an increased height and between 10 or 12 feet apart forming a grid.

A jumping lane, roughly 10 feet wide, running between a double fence either in a straight 50–yard run or in a large circuit, can be used to lay out poles at regular or irregular distances (according to the instructor's whim), to teach the rider to judge distance and stride. This method, and lungeing the horse on the end of a long rein over a grid, can also teach the pupil balance and the forward body position, independent of the reins. Going down the lane in this manner with the arms folded, or hands held above the head, does great things for the rider's balance and increases self-confidence, provided he is not asked to attempt anything too foolhardy.

Once the rider has become adept at negotiating jumps indoors and has outgrown the instructor's imaginative

Riding school manège laid out for jumping practice, showing varying distances between poles and changes of direction.

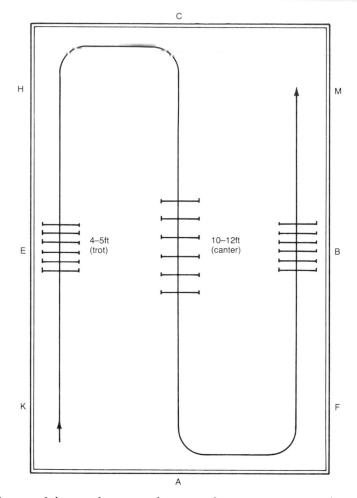

genius and inventiveness, he can then venture out into the paddock with some assurance.

In the paddock, horse and rider can attempt bolder jumps made up from railway sleepers, logs, banks and ditches all designed to be natural to the horse to encourage him to greater exertions. Following these 'natural' obstacles the instructor can begin to use show jumps of various designs and colours, rearranging them often so as to exercise every faculty of the horse and rider.

When jumping, it is essential that riders have sufficient strength in their legs to be able to create impulsion when and where it is needed but unfortunately, regardless of the amount of improvement caused by therapeutic riding and exercises, it is very often impossible to strengthen the legs any more and the seat by itself is not always capable of performing a double task.

Therefore, the rider must be taught to use the so-called 'schooling' whip or shorter whip for jumping, similar to the way in which lady side-saddle riders do, as an extra leg. Pupils must be instructed in the correct method of holding and using it, as well as the time and place, so that it does not frighten or upset the horse at a crucial moment.

Provided the whip is used at the proper time and in a humane way, it will assist the rider to maintain his impetus for the 'lift off'.

It is not advisable, nor in fact is it necessary, to encourage disabled riders to wear spurs at any time, particularly when jumping. It is essential that riders who do have to resort

Introducing trotting poles.

Looking for the next
jump.

to these atrocious objects have sufficient control over the
application of their leg aids to be capable of manipulating
them to a precise degree.

Spare his flanks! He is but flesh and blood and bleeds
like any other!

11 Gymkhana Games

All over the country, from April to September, in mammoth show grounds or on village greens, thousands of young riding enthusiasts hurry to take part in gymkhanas. It is the highlight of the season, something they have worked for hour upon endless hour under the instructor's eagle eye in the riding school or parents' benevolent gaze in the privately owned paddock.

At the gymkhana they meet as in battle and very often a real ding-dong of a battle it is. Ponies oated up to the last grain, highly tuned and straining at the bit, venture out with equally supercharged riders astride, dressed for the fray, ready to wipe the board! It is a wonderfully nerve-racking sight to see, as every shape, size, colour and temperament of pony and rider flash by in deadly but friendly combat.

The air is tense with excitement, tears are many and the language would do credit to the bosun of a tug. At the end of the day comes the journey home, tired but happy, the lucky ones bedecked with clusters of rosettes which will be displayed, talked about and enlarged upon for many a day until the next time. They are the fortunate ones.

Disabled riders (and I mean severely disabled) are not so fortunate. The gymkhana, as we know it, is to them the pot of gold, out of reach except for the very few. They can never hope to compete against riders who have the full use of their limbs and it would be extremely dangerous and stupid to allow or expect them to do so, other than perhaps in leading-rein classes, but even then they would be at an extreme disadvantage.

I do not wish to be misunderstood. I must point out that many disabled riders could and would, if given the opportunity, rush to compete, whatever the strength of the opposition and regardless of the risk involved. The instructor, therefore, must be tactful and sensible in dissuading them, unless of course their disability is so slight that it would make little difference to their chances. However, there is nothing to stop us from holding our own gymkhana or mounted games day for disabled riders and rearranging many of the events and jumping competitions that are normally included in gymkhana schedules.

There is also every good reason for including competitive and non-competitive games in the riding lesson for students who are capable of maintaining a reasonable balance at the walk and trot. Sir Ludwig Guttman, CBE, MD, FRCP, FRCS, former Head Surgeon at the National Spinal Injuries Centre, Stoke Mandeville, pioneer of the Paraplegic Olympic Games and Patron of the Riding for the Disabled Trust stated: 'Competitive sport is not just another means of exercise. The disabled person is continually competing against himself in endurance, quality and performance. To compete against others similarly disabled not only increases the standard of performance and interest in life but also gives a tremendous boost to morale and is psychologically uplifting.'

Riding a horse is, of course, by itself a very intense and strong incentive for the disabled person to achieve the maximum possible physical potential. Both the incentive and desire to improve are increased even more by introducing a competitive element, that becomes extremely motivating and beneficial in a variety of ways. Games, however, do not necessarily have to produce winners; they can be performed just for fun. Instructors must be careful, though, not only with the type of games they devise, but also in their choice of the individual disabled riders who participate. Some emotionally disturbed students may not be capable of withstanding the rigours of competition. Self confidence and self-image must be built up before subjecting this person to such mental pressures. Competitive games must therefore be appropriate for all individual disabled riders in each class.

Games must have a purpose and the instructor should be inventive and enthusiastic in organising those that will motivate and test every individual's abilities to the maximum. For the student to work up to his potential he should enjoy it; therefore the game must be fun and always very active. Instructors should be aware that during games they have the opportunity to observe the students' actual ability and potential. It is noticeable that riders who may be lethargic in the class lesson very often exhibit far more enthusiasm and ability in a game – particularly when they are unaware of being closely observed. Helpers should be reminded that extra exertion and enthusiasm can lead to a sudden loss of balance and coordination, so riders should be watched even more carefully at game time.

Apart from testing the students' mental and physical ability games can be used to test concentration, observation and, in fact, all the senses. Exercises for all disabilities are performed with far more vigour when they form part of a game, and consequently the benefits are enhanced.

Games are normally introduced in the class lesson near the end, after horses have settled and students are relaxed after exertion. Sometimes, however, a game can be introduced early if it encourages a greater response or benefit.

The following is a suggested method for grading physically disabled riders into groups for games:

(1) **Gross** Complete paralysis of limb(s) or a disability so severe as to prevent functional use of the limb(s).
(2) **Severe** A disability which seriously impairs the use of the limb(s), but enables them to be used to some degree functionally.
(3) **Moderate** A disability which only slightly impairs the

functional capacity of a limb or limbs.

(4) **Mild** A disability which is so minimal that the limb or limbs are practically normal.

(5) **Nil** Normal.

Suggested Games and Equipment

The following brief list of games is designed to give the reader some guidelines.

Pole Bending, Hat Race, Cup Race and Hoop-la are all played with bending poles. An inexpensive method of making bending poles is to cement broom handles into large flower pots. These 'potted poles' can then be used either in a game or in the school for an exercise in controlling the horse.

If a single row of four poles is placed down the centre line between markers A and C, approximately ten feet apart, the riders can then be made to weave in and out through the spaces, either in single file or individually. The object is to control and bend the horse without knocking any poles over. The rider should maintain a good balance and firm position throughout without any loss of impulsion.

In gymkhana competitions, four separate rows of poles are used and four competitors at a time race in and out at whatever pace is laid down, returning to the starting point. The first competitor to finish without knocking any poles over is the winner. This competition can also be done as a leading-rein event for less experienced riders and more experienced leaders.

Hat, Cup and Hoop-la races are played by the rider steering the horse at the designed pace, past the poles and dropping either a spare riding hat, paper cup or rubber/plastic ring over the pole and returning to touch the next rider.

'Pole in the Hole' is played by the rider carrying a sawn-off broom handle down and plunging it into the top of a traffic cone, either in lines of four or six, or singly, before

returning to touch the next competitor.

The Potato Race can also be added to the schedule, provided helpers are available to assist the riders. On the starting line, four plastic water buckets are placed on the ground alongside each pony, while at the other end of the arena four helpers hold a number of potatoes.

On the command 'Go' the riders set off for the helper opposite, who hands over the potato. Returning to the start, the competitor drops the potato in the bucket. If he misses the target a helper picks it up and hands it back to the rider to have another try, so that he does not have to dismount to retrieve it. The process is repeated until all the potatoes are dropped in by the winner.

Other games which can be included are 'Post the Letter', 'Washing-line Race', Dressing-up Race', 'Thread the Needle' and 'Musical Sacks', as well as 'Traffic Lights', 'Egg and Spoon' (with plastic egg) and 'Treasure Hunt'.

Straightforward races at the walk, trot and canter, over a measured length between teams are popular. It is up to the instructor in consultation with the physiotherapist, to adapt games so that the rider need not dismount and to use imagin-

Games can be introduced to class lessons to test riders' abilities.

Suggested layouts
for cup races and
bending games.

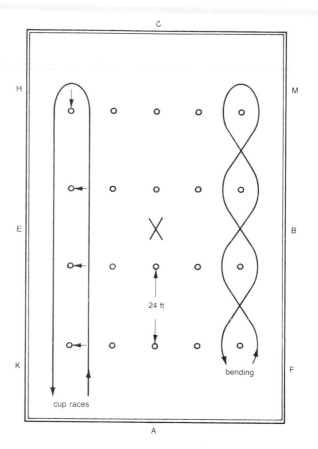

24 ft

bending

cup races

ation in compiling a suitable programme.

Team games are very popular but should be avoided if certain riders, especially cerebral palsy spastic students or those who are emotionally disturbed, become over-excited.

In competitions away from home it is essential that events are judged by a qualified person with a knowledge of the disabilities and experience in teaching the disabled.

Remember also that effort must be rewarded generously, by plenty of praise, particularly for children, and even for those who are not actually placed.

The name of the game is fun!

12 Lungeing and its Benefits

The method of working a horse on a circle, by means of a long webbing rein attached to the front of the lungeing cavesson, is used a great deal in teaching disabled riders, not only in the early stages but periodically throughout their attendance at the centre. This type of training benefits both horse and rider at the same time.

Horses that have been worked for any length of time in the riding school, doing a similar task day after day, tend to become bored and consequently lazy, refusing to respond to the rider, all of which makes the instructor's job as well as the pupil's more difficult. Consequently, short periods on the lunge at frequent intervals, keep the horse supple and obedient to the instructor's voice in the first instance and through that to the rider's aids. It also prevents horses that cannot be made to put sufficient energy into their work, because of the rider's inability, from getting overweight.

When a pupil attends for an individual lesson because he is unable to ride at the same time as a group class, the lungeing of the horse and the instruction of the pupil can be combined with very satisfactory results. Not only can the instructor keep the horse on his toes but, also, he is better able to concentrate more fully on developing the rider's position and balance without being distracted.

A horse being lunged can be used to good effect to demonstrate to an unmounted theory class the different actions at varying paces and over jumps, so they can acquire a knowledge of what goes on 'under the bonnet', which will be of value to them when they are eventually astride.

Exercises performed at all paces on a horse worked in this manner, with and without stirrups or even the saddle, can do much to improve a pupil's seat and balance independently of the reins. The instructor must, of course, ensure that the horse is worked equally on both sides and can, if he so desires, change from the circle and allow the animal to use the full working area, by walking around the school, always keeping the lungeing rein taut, retaining a few loops in the hand to be able to pay out line if required.

Both horse and rider can also derive much physical benefit and confidence from being lunged together over small jumps or cavaletti. A smooth pole or plank should be laid and angled from the ground to the top of the upright or cross on the side that the rein passes over so that the latter runs up and clear without becoming tangled, which could bring down the jump or even the horse and rider as they move up and over.

New horses and ponies recruited for work with disabled riders should be lunged as well as ridden by the instructor (provided they are capable of carrying his weight) so that he can determine and improve upon, if necessary, their standard of education to ensure their suitability. This method of schooling the horse will also get them used to being held by a leader when being ridden and accustom them to their new surroundings and equipment.

In a disabled rider's programme the main advantages are:
(1) Keeping a horse fit when not being ridden.
(2) Instilling confidence in new leaders and helpers.
(3) Remaking older, bored or mishandled horses.
(4) Improving the natural balance and self-carriage.
(5) Introducing the student to a new pace.

Other normal advantages of lungeing that apply are improved conformation and gaits, longitudinal and lateral suppleness, rein contact and transitions. Lungeing is also an excellent method for teaching a less severely physically handicapped student individually or even with a group of students, when there is a shortage of mounts.

The concentration required and the attention received when lungeing, if for only a few brief movements, by an experienced trainer, makes it extremely beneficial.

It is, of course, essential that instructors acquire a complete understanding of the theory and methods of lungeing, for it is by this form of schooling that the trainer makes his first impression on the horse and at this time he should instil the confidence and trust in the new animal which is the foundation of all future discipline and safety.

The equipment that is used for lungeing a disabled student is standard.

(a)   Webbing lunge line with leather stops and quick-release snaps.

(b)   Lungeing cavesson (or correctly fitted snaffle bridle).

(c)   Lunge whip (preferably at least 6 foot).

(d)   Surcingle (with handles and rings for side reins).

(e)   Seat pad (attached to surcingle if required) or thick numnah.

(f)   Side reins (if appropriate) – not for the walk or work over poles or jumps.

13 Vaulting, Back Riding and Driving

Vaulting

Vaulting (the physical act of leaping onto the horse from the ground) is not possible, of course, for the majority of disabled students. However, once mounted with a correctly fitted pad and surcingle, all normal vaulting exercises can be attempted provided they are within the scope of the individual and his disability.

The horse, which should stand between 14hh and 15.2 hh, must be well trained on the lunge, broad backed, with a good temperament and smooth elevated gaits.

Walk and trot are probably the only paces that the majority of disabled students can accomplish alone with confidence at first. This does not prevent others more proficient from attempting and being encouraged to canter at the appropriate time.

Vaulting exercises give a great feeling of self accomplishment and are of tremendous benefit to large numbers of adolescent and younger disabled students who enjoy the opportunity to concentrate on the act of riding without having to physically create the impulsion to drive the horse forwards.

An assistant must always be in attendance throughout the lesson, to give help wherever necessary under the instructor's direction. Signs of fatigue and over-excitement should be anticipated and all safety rules must be observed.

Back riding requires a well trained horse. As a form of therapy it offers many benefits.

Back Riding

Riding 'double' behind the disabled student, or back riding, (as it has become known), is now popular with therapists at some centres.

Sitting close up enables the instructor to offer more support and assistance by the direct 'hands on' method, and he can correct balance, posture, head control and movement quickly.

The warmth and support of the back-rider's body, combined with the horse's rhythmic movement and warmth, has an obvious relaxing effect on the rider, which cannot be exactly duplicated on the bolster in the therapy department.

Students who are recommended for this form of therapy will seldom, if ever, be capable of riding independently. Indeed, it is not the aim of hippotherapy to teach the riding skills. The therapeutic benefits are the primary concern, rather than the desire to produce an accomplished equestrian.

Once again, the excitement and fun of sitting on a live animal is the incentive for accomplishment that is utilised by the therapist, who is always on the lookout for new and more interesting ways to encourgage his patients to maximum effort. The horse is the most recent and most modern discovery, thanks to the equestrian pioneers who founded the movement.

This type of exercise must only be undertaken by a physiotherapist who has the necessary specialised training and is also an experienced rider, with a thorough knowledge and understanding of the horse's paces, temperament and unpredictability.

This 'treatment' should normally only be given on a well-trained, responsive horse, capable of carrying two riders at the walk without objection or discomfort.

A leader and two side walkers may be required at all times in case the horse shies or attempts some other unpredictable evasion.

Back riding can, of course, also be used in the introductory stages for students who are capable of riding progression but may experience some physical inability that can be overcome with this form of assistance.

However, where possible the aim must be towards eventual independent riding. For this type of student the back rider should be an experienced horse person who can take direction from both the therapist and instructor.

Driving

For those disabled would-be equestrians who may be incapable, for various reasons, of riding astride a horse, driving a harness horse from an adapted cart is an ideal substitute. The more elderly disabled in particular, who at an earlier point in time may have driven, might desire to

participate. They should be encouraged to do so and all
normal safety regulations should be observed in making it
possible.

For those who cannot ride astride, driving can provide a good alternative.

A well-trained horse, together with a suitably converted
or standard-type vehicle, with well-fitting harness, must be
utilised. If the cart has to accommodate a wheelchair the
sides must be high enough to prevent it tipping and the
wheels should be secured.

Passengers and drivers with poor balance may require seat
belts or body harnesses with quick-release catches.

Lessons in driving must be given in an enclosed area with
sufficient space for turning and should be under the direct
supervision of an experienced driving instructor at all times.

13 Type and Training of Horse or Pony

The riding school pony has, during the last ten years at least, become a type; in fact, it has very nearly become a breed unto itself, if one mixes with and listens to the old dealers in market yards. 'A good school sort that'n, mate,' is an expression often heard in reference to a particularly stockily built pony. 'Stand up to a fair bit o' pullin' abaht 'e would,' usually follows the first remark, and both comments are well meant and signify a compliment to the animal in question.

It is understandable that this phenomenon should be taking place, when one considers the extraordinary, almost impossible, results that youngsters demand of a pony that they are going to use in riding schools and gymkhana events. He must possess the high-school education of a Schumann horse, the leap and courage of a 'Foxhunter' plus the speed and heart of an 'Arkle', all wrapped up in the frame of a little 13hh Welsh pony.

The dealer, being an old hand at this game, usually convinces the buyer that the sorry little bedraggled pony before him does in fact possess all these attributes and the sale is finalised.

Some months later there is nobody more surprised than the dealer to see at the local gymkhana the remarkable results that can be achieved by hard work and the close association and understanding between a young child and a pony. In fact, the dealer often kicks himself for not asking a higher figure than he did at the sale, without thinking for one minute where the increased credit really lies.

I do not imply by this that proprietors are so demanding in their choice of mounts for use in their riding schools, but they do look for and manage to find among our many native breeds and numerous cross-breeds a type of pony that is capable of giving to some degree an excellent all-round performance.

Before accepting horses and ponies for work with disabled riders, we must be just as dogmatic and equally particular about the type that we require but in a very different way. Not for us the high-spirited, energy-filled pony one can see expertly ridden at the local horse show, although at Chigwell we did in fact keep and use a very fine 16hh thoroughbred horse who was indispensable on the lunge for teaching pupils the finer points of riding, but he was the exception to the rule. What is normally required are horses and ponies that vary in size from 11–15hh, which must have been ridden regularly with sympathy and are proven to be kind in temperament, free and willing movers. They must also be well behaved in the company of their own kind.

What is not required is an animal that is well and truly past his best years, that has any vice such as kicking or biting or that has suffered from or is suffering from any serious complaint, such as laminitis, broken wind or heart trouble, to mention a few.

If it appears that I am trying to give the impression we are looking for a near-perfect pony, well and good, for we are! Isn't everyone? Perfect, that is, for the particular job they require it to do but of course beggars can't be choosers and we often have to make the best of what we have and try to improve upon it.

To illustrate more fully the requirements, I must point out that our pupils come in all shapes and sizes, so obviously we must stable a range of horses and ponies to suit everyone from small children to not-so-small children and adults.

We have not the time, although we may have the facilities

The perfect pony? Cobnut was one of the first ponies at the Diamond Riding Centre in Surrey.

and knowledge, to school or re-school badly handled ponies, therefore it is essential that all animals we take on should have been used and ridden by a competent and knowledgeable rider, so that pupils can learn to ride on a reasonably well-schooled pony that is willing. For this reason, also, horses that are known to possess 'savage elongated molars' or 'telescopic hind legs' (biters and kickers) are not welcomed by either the leaders or grooms, let alone the riders.

As it is unavoidable that ponies are frequently together, both in the school and when out in the grass paddocks, every precaution must be taken to ensure they are compatible.

In the past we were offered, and in fact given by well-meaning friends, horses and ponies that had done their life's work and were due for a well-deserved rest. While not wishing to belittle this kindness and generosity, for which we were most grateful, I must make it clear that a riding centre for the disabled is not a rest home for retired horses. The work they have to do is arduous, at times boring and irritably repetitive, and no amount of sympathy can change that. The lessons and type of exercises are as strenuous, if not more so, as the average riding school's and although we tried to vary the curriculum by hacking them out with able-bodied riders aboard periodically, the pattern of the day-to-day programme did not alter a great deal. Therefore, we should ensure before accepting a gift horse that we do 'look it in the mouth' to avoid being landed with an expensive liability.

General Considerations

Age. The animal should preferably be over five and not aged, with no vices either in the stable or when being ridden. It should be noted that it is considerably more difficult to re-train a horse with bad habits than to train a youngster. 'Old habits die hard' and the older the horse, the more set he is in his ways. There are a few fortunate people who have in fact bred ponies and small horses for use in a handicapped programme, but the time spent with disabled riders is but a small part of their workload. Generally speaking the repetitive, sometimes boring nature of lessons (as far as the horse is concerned) with disabled riders is more suited to a horse or pony that has perhaps 'passed his prime' and is ready for semi-retirement. This does not mean that the older they are, the better. A handicapped rider does not need a handicapped or geriatric horse.

Few programmes will receive gifts of young five-year-olds, unless they breed their own, therefore we must presume that the average age of horses and ponies to be used will be between ten and fifteen years.

This means they may indeed have minds of their own and could have developed some bad habits and a knowledge of how to evade their human keeper's will except when it suits them to obey. Which brings us to our next consideration.

Temperament and Character. As with humans there are good and bad. The bad we have nothing to do with and the good we accept with caution.

Character is important to training and must be summed up in the same way as choosing a friend or even a mate, though of course not for the same reason, or for the same characteristics. Reasonably large ears, a bold eye and a good width of forehead between the eyes are features that particularly suit the equine and denote intelligence plus an ability to respond to fair training. Bad-tempered horses should receive the same treatment as their human counterparts; avoid them!

Horses have good memories; in fact, they rely on them. However, they remember the unpleasant incidents longer than the pleasant ones and how to avoid longer than how to accomplish. Naturally, they will only exert themselves when danger threatens, being by nature timid creatures. A few, however, through modern breeding practices, are not always so timid; in fact they may have complete disrespect for their trainer. This trait will show itself quite early in the formation of temperament and character and they should be approached with caution, whatever the intention of the prospective owner.

Size and conformation are the two other considerations that determine the choice and training required. Some faults in conformation can be corrected, if caught early enough, by careful shoeing and specialised work on the lunge. Horses that 'toe in' or are 'cow-hocked' for instance, can be helped to a degree, but major faults have to be accepted and 'lived with'. The older the horse, the more difficult it is to correct

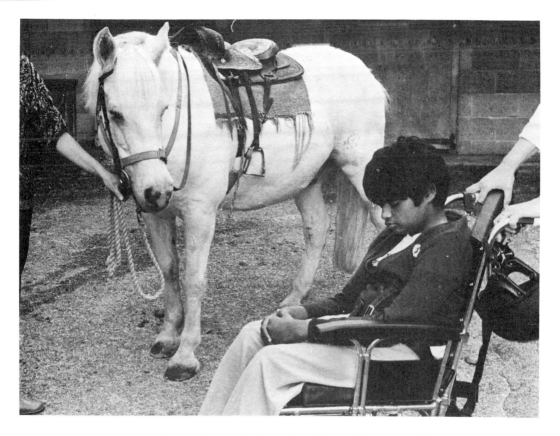

his faults and if the fault is such that it affects the natural action of the horse, the horse should be avoided. Height and width are also to be considered, not only with regard to the selection or suitability for use in a handicapped programme, but also when considering training and schooling.

'I'm ready if you are.' RDA ponies must be both kind and willing.

It is obvious that a horse over 15.2hh makes it very difficult for a sidewalker to assist the rider. Similarly, a wide-backed animal presents difficulties for the cerebral palsy rider, with tight adduction in the legs.

A different approach is also required with respect to the training of larger horses and smaller ponies. One should never underestimate the power of the pony, many breeds of which have distinct minds of their own and resent the human intrusion into their everyday routine. The more settled they are into a certain pattern, developed by a single child owner over a period of years, the less likely they are to change.

Some breeds of horses other than the thoroughbred (whom we all know has a mind of its own), also exhibit certain traits that must be carefully weighed against the breed and the cost of re-training.

The type of student the group intends to recruit will determine the size of the mount.

Gaits. The gait or pace of the horse or pony differs greatly of course, and will influence the training required. It is essential, however, that those chosen for work with the disabled have good natural forward movement (that should be unhindered by the leader), plus smooth transitions up and down from walk to canter. The emphasis as always is safety, which can be almost guaranteed by a smooth action, and rider comfort. Again it is possible to improve gaits with specialised training such as lungeing and long-reining.

Acclimatising and Training the Horse

In spite of, or because of, the aforementioned it is presumed that horses accepted for the programme have been correctly backed, bitted and handled, regularly ridden by a competent rider with no major vices and are serviceably sound. This being the case I will comment now on the specialised training required and make reference to the basic equestrian training methods only where they are applicable.

The introduction of the horse to the peculiarities of a riding for the handicapped programme may take some time, but it is essential that the initial trial period is not rushed.

There are a number of unusual objects that will never have been encountered before and even a number of quaint people that are not normally found in the average riding stable.

Mounting Ramps, Wheelchairs etc. Probably the most strange to the horse, and the one that will require some getting used to, is the mounting ramp. Ramps do vary from programme to programme as far as height, width and materials. Some are single, others double-sided, made of wooden planks, tubular steel or even plywood. They are particularly frightening to the new horses.

Time and patience must be spent letting the mount walk around, or through it and even feeding him by it if necessary, before letting anyone walk on it. Having a human stomping around higher than his head is not an everyday occurance that is taken lightly. Gradually, however, assistants can move about on top of and up the ramp on both sides of the horse, while the leader reassures and steadies him. This period must not be rushed if the experience is to be of any value at all later on. Once people are accepted without concern the heavier equipment can be brought in. Wheelchairs, walking frames and crutches are far beyond the average horse's comprehensions and the noise and the feel of them instils a desire to flee. Be that as it may, we must continue, by gentle persuasion and firm insistence, to encourage indifferent acceptance.

Spinning the wheels around on top of the platform, letting crutches fall, and clanking up and down the slope with a walking frame, until the horse registers complete and utter boredom, is the only possible method. Letting these same articles actually touch the sides of the horse or any other part of his anatomy, could of course, send him into a quivering jellied mass. However, perseverance will win in the end and one only has to keep poking away, as they say, to obtain the desired response. Eventually the horse will stand immobile while all around him is in bedlam.

In the act of mounting a disabled rider it is not unusual to observe one or two helpers (or even a therapist) also draped over the horse in various poses of languishment, desperately trying to extricate themselves from beneath the weight of the student, who is invariably totally unaware of their predicament and incapable of assisting anyway. Not infrequently has my head been pinned by a vice-like involuntary grip to the saddle by a student's arm, or received a sharp undercut under the jaw from a spasmodic twitch of the knee.

Not only does the horse have to stand calm while all about him appears in disarray, but leaders and assistants also require training and a measure of self-control and humour to pull them through.

Eventually, after a suitable period of trial, vet checks, and becoming accustomed to his new surroundings the horse or pony will be accepted. It is at this moment that the real period of training and discovery begins. For perhaps five or maybe even ten years of its life this equine has been handled, petted, lead and mounted always from the left (or near) side. Suddenly, a bebaubled bunch of flowingly garbed, perfumed women may rush up on the off-side and try to deposit a kicking screaming, incoherent, steel-clad bundle onto his back from the 'wrong' side. It blows his mind!

The horse must be trained to accept a rider being mounted and dismounted from both sides and by a greater variety of methods than those normally used in the show ring.

Similarly, being led from both sides and in both directions takes time to accept and to follow: 'Old habits die hard.'

Sidewalkers. Sidewalkers are another thing to contend with. The poor old horse by nature is, I believe, claustrophobic. To be hemmed in on both sides by humans and restricted to such a narrow path (known as the track) must really try the patience of our noblest and long-suffering friend. Of all the things that the horse finds the most difficulty in coping with in his new environment, it is perhaps the sidewalker. Without so much as a 'by your leave?' or 'may I?' they lean all over his loins with their sharp elbows, drag on the stirrups and even have the audacity to tell the leader to 'slow down!' just when the horse has found a good rhythmic stride.

They do, of course, as we all know, have their uses, one of which is to try and ensure that the student remains in the semblance of a central position, so that the weight remains constant.

Unequal distribution of weight and sudden body or limb movements take a while for the horse to become accustomed to, particularly if the limb happens to bear a brace. To know when to react and when not to react to the touch of steel, or a sudden thrust forward is a lesson that will take much time and patience to teach.

Exercises that involve sudden movements and unusually large numbers of people around, tend also to fuss the new horse and cause some concern. Practised stationary at first by an able rider and then on the move with a leader, produces results.

Equipment. The same applies to equipment used in games and competitions. Familiarisation and rehearsals with volunteer 'pony clubbers' and the like will ensure safety of all.

The use of 'special' riding equipment also requires a brief period of training to accustom the horse to the unusual feel of the article and its meaning, which may not be quite the same as standard items. The double lead line attached to the rings of the bit and the ladder or looped reins have a very different feel and affect the horse in a much more direct way than the standard items.

Breaking in. It is essential that every horse is ridden by a competent person to determine its knowledge of the aids for both diagonal and simple lateral movements, at the three basic paces. If the horse has been ridden by any other method than basic English, he may have to be re-trained and put to the aids again, to ensure he understands the commands of the student (however ineffective they may be).

It is not unusual to have horses, and particularly ponies, that have never been ridden indoors or are totally unfamiliar with any type of enclosed arena. They may at first be petrified by an indoor school. It takes time and perseverance to overcome the natural instincts to run for the exit or herd to some new-found equine friends.

An older, more experienced horse that has been in the programme for a while can be invaluable in calming the newcomer's fears.

The voice of the trainer or instructor takes on a new significance when teaching the class lesson of disabled students.

On the lunge, the horse learned to respond to tone and inflections, and this can be carried over into the actual class. A well-timed 'Whoa' or a sharp 'Trot on!' can be of invaluable assistance to both students and leaders, particularly when difficulties occur.

The horse used for the disabled must respond to the voice in almost an identical a manner as circus-trained horses. Corrections and reward are made more powerful and effective tools by the use of the voice.

Positioning, long-reining, and loose schooling are other, more sophisticated methods of training or exercising the horse. They not only teach him to obey verbal commands, but also make the animal aware of the position of the instructor and simple physical movements and commands that become part of his understanding and obedience.

Every instructor should be aware, at all times, of his position with regard to horse and rider and the exact directions and pace that he wants them to proceed at. A knowledge of where to be and at what time is probably the largest single safety factor in the trainer's or instructor's repertoire.

Feeding. A word about feeding versus work. Large

amounts of grain or corn should be avoided for the average horse or pony that will be used in the programme. Feed according to the work and only increase the grain as the frequency and nature of work demands it.

Hacking out and taking part in competitions away from home can add variety to a pony's workload.

It is obvious that horses used exclusively for the disabled do not receive the amounts of vigorous exercise or intense training of the average equestrian centre horse. Therefore it is imperative, as already stated, that they are regularly ridden by able riders, who break the monotony of lessons by hacking out or competing in small shows, or even hill-topping at the local hunt, to keep them from becoming stale. Alternatively, a regular turn-out to play in a good shaded pasture, where they can kick up their heels and give vent to their feelings, will produce a far better animal for a much longer period.

Type. I would not attempt to specify which native breed is most suitable for work of this kind, because in riding schools all over the country one could probably single out every known breed, each doing a similarly worthwhile job.

Being situated in the south of England, however, we naturally came across and were offered more New Forest, Welsh and Moorland ponies more than any others. We also possessed some excellent ponies of doubtful parentage, as well as breeds crossed with the Arab and thoroughbred, plus a really honest character from Ireland.

Whatever the breed or type, let us remember it is the horse's broad back that bears the weight and he is primarily the healer – once again, even in this age of the rocket, proving his worth. Without him there would be no riding for the disabled.

Postscript

Where Do We Go From Here?

There is still some difficulty in knowing how to conclude this book: even now, twenty years after it was first published, we are still learning, still developing new equipment and exploring new methods, exactly as we did in the beginning. The difference now is that we have access to the vast experiences and knowledge gained from those years and those pioneers who laid the foundations.

At Chigwell we proved over and over again that it worked: a nine-year-old Cockney child once crawled on her hands and knees to her pony and eventually not only cantered and jumped it but walked completely unaided when off the pony; a twenty-year old polio victim could not stand without a frame when he first came to ride, but finally walked on elbow crutches the length of Britain and across the United States to set a world record – but that is another story . . .

These were two from thousands who were and still are being given the opportunity to prove their right to exist in a world that is all-too-often inclined, even today, to look the other way. It has been achieved without miracles but by courage, commonsense, devotion and hard work. Great advances have been made in evaluation, teaching techniques and the therapeutic approach to riding for the disabled.

Most western nations and some countries behind the Iron Curtain now have national organisations that administer hundreds of centres with thousands of participants who enjoy 'the sport of kings'. Riding a horse or pony is without doubt an activity that is accepted and here to stay for so many disabled individuals, who may never have realised the opportunity to enjoy the freedom and exhilaration of the sport if it hadn't been for those few, who in the beginning, believed in what they were doing.

It is no longer necessary to prove the concept, it is time to improve it. Hippotherapy is now prescribed as a modern acceptable form of treatment for a multitude of disabilities by doctors, surgeons and therapists with the same assurance as hydrotherapy was prescribed twenty years ago.

Riding for the disabled is, without doubt, here to stay and if by writing this book I have contributed in some small way to this, then it has certainly been worthwhile.

Rastus, waiting for his master.

I Can

I cannot walk or run, or play
a game of tennis every day.
I cannot dance or ride a bike,
I'll never know what skating's like.
I have no soccer boots or ball,
they are no use to me at all.
I'll never ski the waves or snow,
so many thrills I'll never know.
I'll never sail the wind or surf
or chase a ball across the turf,
nor climb the snow-capped peaks above,
so many things I'll never love.
But I can ride through forest trails
to see the fox and rabbits' tails
and watch the geese and ducks take flight
while leaping stags and deer take fright.
And I can follow mountain tracks
past climbers weighted down with packs,
to trace a river to its source
astride the broad back of a horse.
Yes I enjoy the 'sport of kings'
when carried high my feet take wings.
To fly me on a pleasure course,
for I can mount and ride a horse.

John Anthony Davies

(Dedicated to the Canadian Therapeutic Riding Association)

Bibliography

The Art of Lungeing, Sylvia Stanier, J.A. Allen & Co., London.

Basic Equitation, Jean Licart, J.A. Allen & Co., London.

The Cerebral Palsied Rider, (Pony Riding for the Disabled Trust) Doreen Allen, MCSP, Dip. TP.

The Developmental Progress of Infants, Her Majesty's Stationery Office, London.

The Handbook, North American Riding for the Handicapped Assoc.

The Instructor's Handbook, The British Horse Society.

Lifting Patients in the Home, The Chartered Society of Physiotherapy.

Manual of Horsemanship, The British Horse Society.

Mounted Games, The British Horse Society.

Risk Exercise and the Handicapped, Dr Sol Roy Rosenthal, MD, Ph.D.

Teaching Basic Riding, Anne Lewis, J.A. Allen & Co., London

Teaching the Child Rider, Pamela Roberts, J.A. Allen & Co., London.

Your Horse and His Care, A. Prentice, MBE, AM Inst.

Index

Page numbers in *italics* indicate illustration.